Prepared during the International Year of the Child and dedicated to all children for whom play is the very essence of life.

IMPROVISED PLAY THINGS

MARGARET ELLIS AND A. BRIAN NIELSEN

THE UNIVERSITY OF ALBERTA PRESS

First published by
The University of Alberta Press
Edmonton, Alberta, Canada
1980

ISBN 0-88864-062-5

Ellis, Margaret, 1932-
  Improvised playthings

ISBN 0-88864-062-5

  1. Toy making—Amateurs' manuals.
2. Playgrounds—Apparatus and equipment.
I. Nielsen, A. Brian, 1950-   II. Title.
TT174.E44   745.592   C80-091003-6

Printed by John Deyell Company,
Willowdale, Ontario, Canada.

Contents

Acknowledgements

Most of the equipment described in this manual was designed by the authors and constructed by Mr. Earle Dallyn or the authors. Some of the pieces were designed and made by students in MOV 433—Movement Education for Young Children—at the University of Alberta. Grateful thanks are extended to all of the above. A special acknowledgement is due Brenda Lovell who spent many hours writing out and sketching construction ideas for the small manipulative equipment. It would be impossible to thank individually everyone who contributed suggestions, ideas, or actual designs appearing in the manual, but we would like these people to know that their interest and assistance is greatly appreciated and was taken into consideration.

Compilation of this material was made possible by a grant from Recreation, Parks, and Wildlife, Government of Alberta.

Introduction

If you've ever faced a group of enthusiastic children and wanted to direct all that energy into positive channels, this is the manual for you. In the pages which follow you will find a wide variety of play equipment designed to challenge and stimulate children. Build each item at home or in class, experiment with each, and watch the children invent new ways to use the equipment. But before you begin, there are several basic principles you should keep in mind.

All the equipment in this manual has been used by children in movement programs and there has been no incidence of equipment failure to the authors' knowledge. However, the authors take no responsibility for the safety of children while using equipment made to these specifications. Play equipment, whether it is homemade or professionally engineered, must be durable, safe, attractive, and varied.

Durability

The materials and construction methods suggested in the manual should be closely followed since the playthings you build will receive long, hard use from the children. We have suggested you use plywood in most cases because it is the strongest, lightest, and most easily handled material. It is particularly useful for large, flat surfaces. Particle board is heavier, less resilient, and does not hold nails or screws well.

Your homemade structures will be more durable if you take the time to both nail and glue all joints. White glue is adequate for joins where little stress is involved. However, the strongest glue for wood to wood bonding is one of the resorcinol or formaldehyde adhesives. Additionally, resorcinol glues are fully waterproof. Both require clamping for three to ten hours during setting. Where the wood is thick, it is better to use screws in place of nails. If you need to make several joins during the construction of your play equipment, be sure to use a T-square or a ply square when measuring. Precision will increase the durability of your products.

Safety

With young children, safety is as important as durability. All nail, screw, and bolt heads must be countersunk and the holes filled with plastic wood. Cracks, knots, and other irregularities should also be filled. Wood surfaces must be carefully sanded smooth before painting to ensure they will be splinter-free. Edges and corners must be rounded or padded. Materials used for finishing, such as

1

paint, varnish, and marking pens, must be non-toxic, especially on equipment used by very young children.

As a general precaution, you should provide equipment which is scaled to the size of the children using it. Once your program is established, allow the children to proceed at their own individual paces. As for maintenance, as soon as the equipment shows signs of wear, remove it from the play area until it can be properly repaired. Wash the pieces thoroughly at least once a month.

Attractiveness

Although the basic materials of the equipment may be recycled ones, you should give very careful thought and attention to finishing the pieces attractively so they are transformed into new creations visually as well as functionally. The drawings and text give some suggestions for design, but much is left up to your own imagination. Since children unconsciously begin to form their early aesthetic values from the structure, colour, texture, and design of their playthings, your decisions in this area should be well informed ones.

Variety

Variety is one of the most important elements in an effective play program. Use the manual to select a range of equipment which will offer varied experiences requiring balance, co-ordination, flexibility, and endurance. Try involving the children when it is time to plan new equipment, and once your selections are made vary your gym or home layout regularly to encourage fresh ideas from the children who use it. If you provide some light, moveable pieces, the children will be able to create their own environment.

In the pages which follow, you will find instructions to help you create strong and useful play equipment. Most of the pieces can be used outdoors or indoors in the gym, the classroom, or the home. All of them are easy to make and require no unusual tools or carpentry skills. Perhaps more importantly, each piece described has been tested by children and has been modified to improve its play value.

The main advantages of homemade structures are that they can be inexpensively made, easily repaired, individually styled, and designed to meet particular needs. Many throw-away items, such as tires, inner tubes, appliance boxes, cans, and scrap lumber, can be obtained from garages, lumber yards, construction sites, telephone companies, and junk yards at little or no cost. Also, the children can bring materials from home and become involved in the creative process.

To simplify your search for the right piece of equipment we have divided the manual into eleven sections, each dealing with a different type of equipment. Each item is separately described and illustrated under three headings: materials, construction, and variations. In many cases suggestions for use are made and cross-references to other items are included to suggest suitable combinations, and on many pages space is provided so that notes can be made of your own ideas about and modifications to the equipment.

We believe that homemade play equipment is an economical alternative to expensive manufactured items. Furthermore, when adults and children work together to create play equipment, the process itself has advantages. It brings adults and children together in joint projects and allows each to grow through the experience. It develops skills in both age groups and fosters common participation in the excitement of growing up. We hope you will use this manual as an avenue to exploration and fun with your children.

Notes on wood measurements

When you use *finished hardwood* keep in mind that "stock sizes" are not the same as the actual measurements, as the following lists demonstrates:

stock size	actual dimensions
1×1	¾ in. × ¾ in.
1×2	¾ in. × 1½ in.
1×3	¾ in. × 2½ in.
1×4	¾ in. × 3½ in.
2×2	1½ in. × 1½ in.
2×3	1½ in. × 2½ in.
2×4	1½ in. × 3½ in.

Additionally, since *plywood* is now cut and sold in metric units, you must allow for a reduction in thickness of 1/16 inch; for example, 5/8 in. (10/16 in.) plywood now measures 9/16 in. thick. *To avoid errors always measure wood carefully before cutting.*

In this manual all measurements are given in feet and inches. However, should you wish to use the metric scale, here are some basic conversions:

1 inch = 2.54 cm = 25.4 mm
1 foot = 30.48 cm = 304.8 mm
1 yard = 91.44 cm = 914.4 mm

Stocking ball

Supplies

Materials
newspaper or paper towels
a nylon knee-high stocking
thread

Tools
needle

Construction

Dampen the paper and shape into a ball (the tighter this ball, the harder the finished one will be). Stuff the paper ball into the toe of the stocking. Twist the stocking at the top of the ball to close the opening (diagram a). Push the ball into the remaining leg section of the stocking and twist again (diagram b). Repeat until all of the stocking is around the ball (ensure the twists are not above one another). Sew the end of the stocking to the ball to prevent it unwrapping.

Variations

Materials
Use different fillings, such as nylon hose or fabric.

Construction
Dye the stockings before use.
Add embroidery to the outside.
Attach a piece of elastic to the ball for suspension or for batting (see pp. 12-20).
Size
Vary the size of the original paper ball.

a

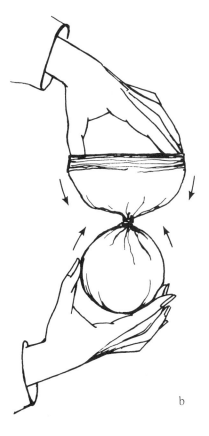

b

Foam ball

Supplies

Materials
foam—a piece of 12 in. × 18 in. × ½ in. thick foam
heavy-duty thread

Tools
cardboard for template, scissors, large needle

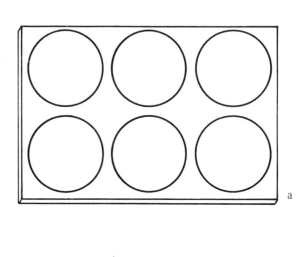

Construction

Cut a 6 in. diameter circle from the cardboard. Place this template on the foam, mark, then cut six circles (diagram a). Select one circle and draw a line dividing the circle in half. Stack the six circles with the marked circle on top. Following the dividing line, sew all six pieces of foam together (diagram b). Pull the thread as tight as possible on each stitch and continue all the way along the line with ⅜ in. stitches. A back stitch will make a firm join and prevent the thread from pulling through. When the stitching is complete, the ball will fan out forming a rounded shape (diagram c).

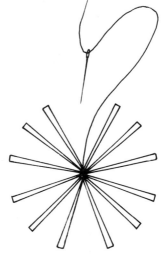
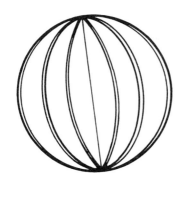

Variations

Materials
Use variously coloured foam.

Construction
Use a staple gun to fasten the pieces of foam together instead of the thread.

Size and shape
Vary the foam thickness from ¼ in to 1 in. This will increase or decrease the number of layers.
Make the circles larger or smaller.
Vary the shape of the foam pieces to an oval (diagram d).

Small foam balls can be used with **Scoops,** p. 17, or nylon stocking bats, pp. 12-14.

Yarn ball

Supplies

Materials
yarn—2 to 3 ounces of heavy yarn
cardboard—two 6 in. × 6 in. pieces of cardboard
string—one 9 in. piece of string

Tools
scissors, needle

Construction

Cut two 6 in. diameter circles. In the centre of each circle cut a 2 in. hole (diagram a). Place the two cardboard pieces together. Wrap the yarn continuously through the hole in the centre and around the outer perimeter. Pull the yarn tight as it is wrapped (diagram b). Continue the wrapping until the cardboard is thickly covered and the hole in the centre is filled (diagram c). A needle will be needed to pull the yarn through when the hole becomes very small. With scissors, cut all the layers of yarn along the outer edge of the circle between the two cardboard pieces (diagram c). Slide the string between the cardboards and tie tightly and securely (diagram d). Cut and remove the cardboard. Fluff out the ball and trim if necessary.

Variations

Materials
Use scraps of wool tied together.
Use different thicknesses of wool.
Use different coloured yarn for each ball, or within each ball for multicoloured balls.

Construction
When first winding put several threads together to shorten the winding time.
Attach a long string or elastic to the ball.
Size
Vary the diameter of the cardboard circles—10 in. for a large ball, 3 in. for a small ball.

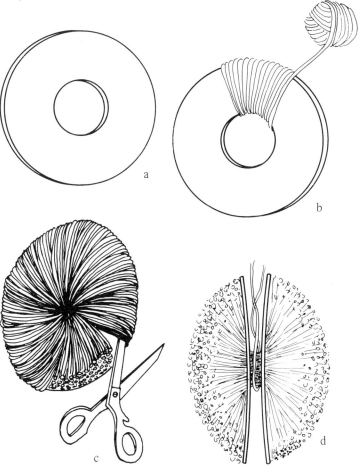

7

Fabric ball

Supplies

Materials
paper—from a brown-paper bag
fabric—¾ yard of sturdy fabric
foam rubber chips
thread

Tools
pins, scissors, sewing machine, needle

Construction

Make the paper pattern (diagram a). Pin the pattern to the fabric. Cut out six panels. Place the right sides of the panels together for stitching. Sew the panels together with a double row of stitching, allowing for a ½ in. seam (diagram b). Leave a 4 in. opening in the last seam. Clip seams close to the stitching and iron the seams open (diagram c). Turn the cover right side out. Fill the ball with foam rubber chips until the ball takes on a firm, round appearance (diagram d). Close the opening with hand stitching.

Variations

Materials
Vary the colour of the fabric.
Use cut up hose as filling.
Construction
Decorate with embroidery (diagram e).
Size and shape
Vary the size and shape of the ball.
Vary the shape of the panels—take a pattern from a commercial ball, such as a baseball (diagram f).

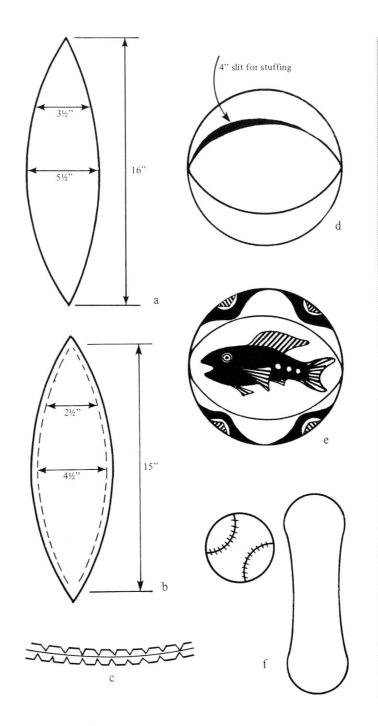

8

Step-and-swing ball

Supplies

Materials
one 18 in. length of strong cord
old tennis ball
swivel hook and ring
plastic bleach bottle
adhesive tape—cloth or coloured

Tools
scissors or sharp knife, punch or stout nail (to make hole in plastic ring), large canvas needle

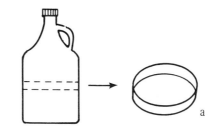

Construction

Cut a 1½ in. strip from a 6 in. diameter plastic bottle (diagram a). If the ring needs to be smaller, cut out a section, overlap the ends, and tape the edges. Bind the entire plastic ring with tape. Pierce a hole in the ring, thread the cord through, and knot the end inside the ring (diagram b). Cut the cord 6 to 8 in. long outside the ring. Attach a swivel hook to one end of the cord and a metal ring to the other section of cut cord (diagrams b, c). Thread the second end of the cut section through the ball and knot securely (diagram c).

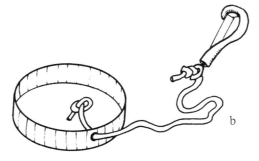

Variations

Construction
Use only a rope or cord and ball. Make a loop at the end of the rope for the leg.

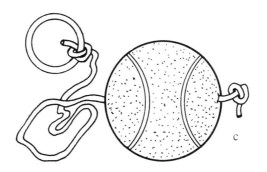

Ring

Supplies

Materials
plastic hose or tubing—one 18 in. length of ¾ in. (inside diameter) rubber or plastic hose
wood—3 in. of ¾ in. dowel
staples
adhesive tape
wood glue

Tools
sharp knife

Construction

Cut the ends of the hose at a slight angle with the outside edge longer than the inside edge (diagram a). Heat the ends of the plastic hose (to expand the opening). Dip the ends of the dowel into glue. Push the dowel into the ends of the hose, ensuring the ends fit tightly together. Staple through the hose into the dowel. Tape over the join (diagram b).

Variations
Materials
Vary the colour of the tubing.
Vary the firmness or flexibility of the hose.
Make the ring from rope.
Cut styrofoam in a flat circle.
Construction
Cover the completed ring with yarn or tape, especially if hose is not firm enough (diagram c).
Size
Vary the diameter of the ring according to its use.

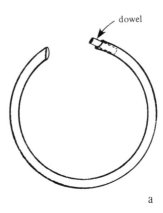

dowel

a

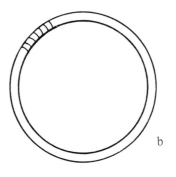

b

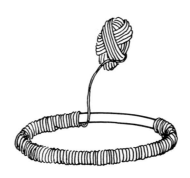

c

tape

rope

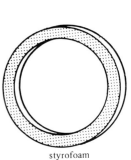

styrofoam

Birdie

Supplies

Materials
cork—1 in. to 1½ in. cork
duck or other suitable feathers
masking tape

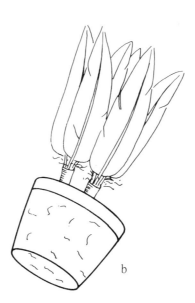

Construction

Tape the feathers together in small clusters (diagram a),
then tape these clusters close together around the edge of
the cork (diagram b). Continue until the cork is completely circled (diagram c).

Variations

Materials
Use a small ball, table tennis or practice golf ball, instead of
the cork.
Construction
Tape the complete cork to give more weight and durability to
the hitting end.
Place the feathers close together around the edge before taping
rather than binding them together in clusters.

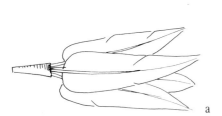

2 Bats and scoops

Hanger hose bat

Supplies

Materials
metal coat hanger
stocking leg
string
tape—athletic or adhesive

Construction

Bend the hanger into a diamond shape, or a shape of your choice (diagram a). Straighten the hook and bend it in half toward the wire joint. Push the wire shape into the stocking, making sure the shape fits snugly into the toe of the stocking. Pull the stocking tightly around the hanger. Gather the excess stocking and bind it to the handle with string. Tape the entire handle.

Variations

Construction
Dye the stocking different colours.
Draw a pattern on the bat (diagram b).
Use two stockings for greater strength.
Place tape around the perimeter of the bat for extra strength.
Bind the straightened hook with another stocking to make a longer handle.

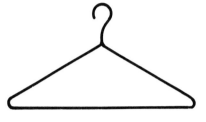

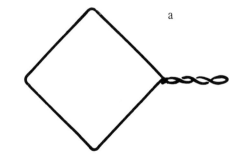

a

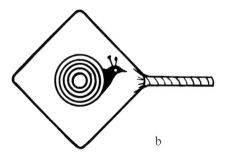

b

This bat is best used with lightweight balls and other objects made of paper, styrofoam, yarn, or rubber foam.

Bat-a-ball

Supplies

Materials
metal hanger
stocking leg
string
tape
thread
cardboard—two thin 1 in. squares with a hole in the
    centre
small foam or yarn ball—1½ in. to 2 in. diameter
elastic—one 12 to 18 in. length of thin elastic
glue

Tools
large-eyed needle

Construction

Make the bat as for **Hanger hose bat,** p. 12. Thread the elastic strip through the eye of the needle and then pass the needle and the elastic through the centre of the ball. Tie a knot in the end of the elastic. Glue the two cardboard squares to opposite sides of the centre of the bat. Allow to dry thoroughly before continuing. Thread the elastic through the centre hole, pushing it through the hose. Remove needle and tie a knot in the elastic.

Variations

Materials
The bat can be made of plywood with an attached rubber ball.

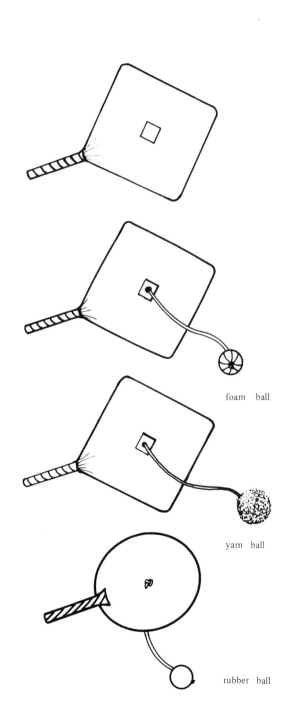

foam ball

yarn ball

rubber ball

13

Wire hose bat

Supplies

Materials

wood—one 4 in. length of 1 in. dowel
wire—40 in. of No. 10 wire
stocking—one good leg of sandalfoot hose
glue
thread
paint or varnish
wax crayon

Tools

broom handle, file, drill, hammer, sandpaper

Construction

Bend the wire into the desired shape. Use a broom handle
to smooth and round the corners. File the wire ends to a
sharp point. Drill two holes, side by side, in the end of
the dowel. These should be slightly smaller than the diameter of the wire and 1 in. deep. Put glue into the holes,
insert the wire ends, and tap gently into place with a
hammer (diagram a). Sand the edges and ends of the
wooden handle, then paint or varnish. Pull the stocking
over the wire frame until it fits snugly. Gather the excess
nylon around the wire at the base of the frame and glue
and tie securely. Draw a pattern on the nylon with a wax
crayon, felt pen, or paint (diagram b).

Variations

Materials

Use a coloured stocking or dye the stocking a variety of
colours.
Use heavy-duty hose.

Construction

Use a different strength wire.
Vary the handle width and length depending on the child's age
and size.
Use two or three thicknesses of hose.
Place tape around the perimeter of the bat for added protec-
tion.

Size and shape

Vary the shape and size of the bat (diagram c).

Do not use this bat on the floor unless the edges are rein-
forced. Use only with a light ball.

Wooden bat

Supplies

Materials

wood—one 8 in. × 14 in. piece of ⅜ in. plywood
   —one 14 in. length of ½ in. × 1½ in. hardwood
    (or same length of 1½ in. diameter half-round)
wood glue
paint or varnish

Tools

jig- or sabre saw, rasps, sandpaper, paintbrush

Construction

Mark an 8 in. diameter circle on the plywood at one end. Then mark a handle 6 in. long and 1½ in. wide from the base of the circle (diagram a). Cut out the bat and handle shape in one piece. Cut the 14 in. hardwood in half yielding two 7 in. lengths. Rasp, hone, and sand each 7 in. block to a rounded, graduated surface ⅛ in. thick at one end and ¼ in. thick at the other. The 1½ in. side must stay flat (diagram b). Glue the hardwood pieces to opposite sides of the bat handle shape. With the ends flush, the hardwood pieces extend 1 in. onto the bat face (diagram c). If you are using half-round, you need only taper, with the rasp, the end overlapping the bat face. Sand thoroughly and paint or varnish.

Variations

Materials

If the hardwood pieces are eliminated, the handle is not as strong, but the bat is lighter.
Use adhesive tape to further bind the handles.

Construction

Drill holes in the bat surface to reduce air resistance.
Paint pictures on the bat surface.

Size and shape

Ovals, circles, squares, and rectangles are all suitable shapes.
Vary the handle length and thickness to suit the children using the bats.
Vary the thickness of the plywood.

This bat should be used with light- and medium-weight balls.

c

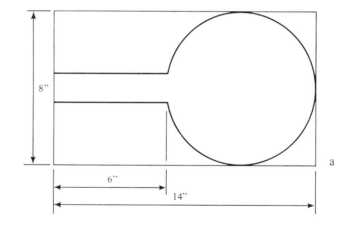

8"

6"

14"

a

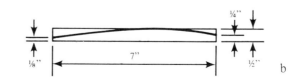

¼"

⅛"

7"

½"

b

Newspaper bat

Supplies

Materials
wood—one 2 ft. length of 1 in. dowel
cardboard tube—1 ft. long × 1½ in. diameter
newspaper
masking tape
staples
glue
paint

Tools
scissors, staple gun, paintbrush

Construction

Wrap newspaper tightly around 12 in. of the dowel until it fits snugly into the tube (diagram a), then glue this wrapped end into the cardboard tubing. Cut twelve 10 in. diameter circles from the newspaper. Cut 4 in. slits from opposite directions toward the circle centres (diagram b). Centre and wrap these sheets over the end of the tubing and tape in place (diagram c). Prepare twelve sheets of newspaper as shown (diagram d). Roll these sheets around the tubing from corner to corner and secure each sheet with tape. Tape the last layer on with diagonal strips (diagram e). Staple one edge of the newspaper to the dowel and the other end to the tube. Paint and decorate (diagram f).

Variations

Materials
Replace newspapers with large sheets of wrapping paper.

Construction
For additional strength, dip newspaper in wallpaper paste before wrapping.
Size
Vary the handle size and length.
Increase the batting surface by using a larger tube.

Use this bat with lightweight objects, such as the **Stocking ball,** p. 5; **Yarn ball,** p. 7; and **Foam ball,** p. 6.

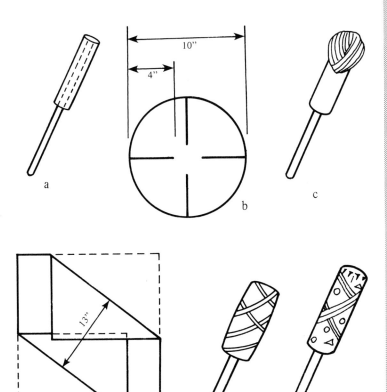

a   10"   4"   b   c

d   e   f

Scoop

Supplies

Materials
plastic vinegar or bleach bottle with handle
paint

Tools
scissors or sharp knife, sandpaper, paintbrush

Construction

Remove the bottom and part of the side of the bottle
above the handle with a sharp knife or scissors (diagram
a). Round all corners and sand edges smooth (diagram
b). Rinse the bottle thoroughly, dry, and paint.

Variations

Materials
Any plastic bottle can be used providing it has a handle.
Construction
Make a variety of opening sizes and positions (diagram c).
Tape around the cut edge with electrician's or masking tape.
Attach a lightweight ball or cork to a length of yarn, placing
the other end of the yarn between the bottle neck and the cap
(diagram d).
Attach a dowel or broomstick handle into the neck of a bottle
without a handle (diagram e).

The location of the cutout portion of the scoop with re-
spect to the handle will determine what types of actions
are encouraged. For beginners, the cutout may be best located on the same side as the handle.

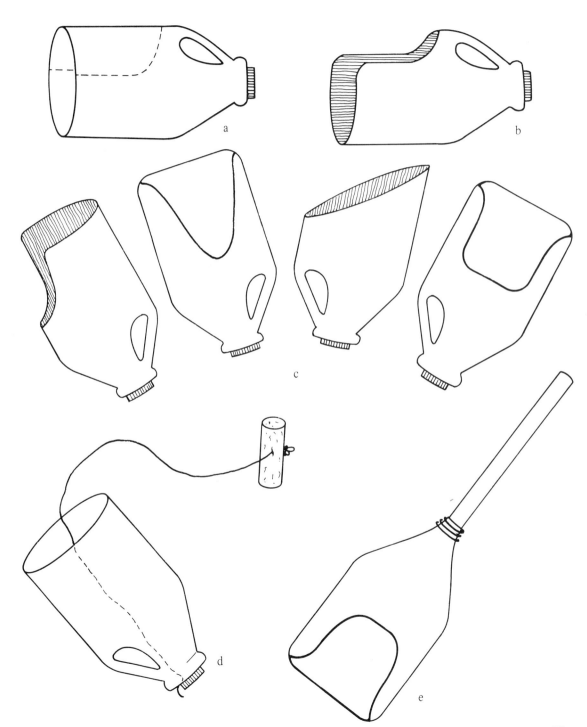

Flip-it

Supplies

Materials

wood—two 14 in. lengths of ⅜ in. dowel
fabric—one piece 14 in. × 10 in.
elastic—20 in. piece of hat or other thin elastic
staples
thread
paint

Tools

sandpaper, scissors, sewing machine, large-eyed needle
or large bobby pin, staple gun, paintbrush

Construction

Round both ends of each dowel rod, sand, and paint.
Make a ¼ in. hem along each 14 in. side of the material.
Cut the elastic into two 10 in. pieces and thread one
through each ¼ in. hem. Attach securely at the ends.
Note: the elastic must be shorter than the material. Make
a ½ in. hem along the 10 in. sides of the material, stitching close to the edge (diagram a). Slide a dowel through
each ½ in. hem so that one end just shows (diagram b).
Attach the material to the dowel from top to bottom with
staples.

Variations

Materials

Use a longer length of dowel.
Use strong netting instead of material.

Construction

The net or material can be stapled directly to the dowel instead
of making a hem to hold it.

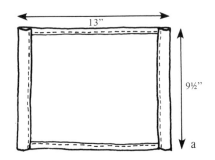

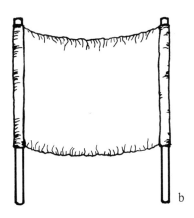

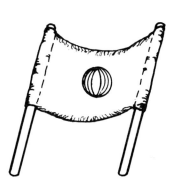

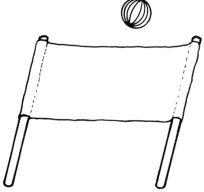

Stamp-it-up

Supplies

Materials
wood—one 5 in. × 20 in. piece of ⅜ in. plywood or
      hardwood (board)
      —one 5 in. length of 1 ×2 hardwood (base)
screws—three ¾ in. wood screws
wood glue
wood filler
paint

Tools
drill, screwdriver, putty knife, sandpaper, paintbrush

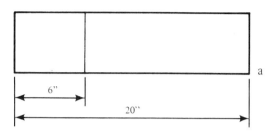

a

Construction

Draw a line across the plywood 6 in. from one end (diagram a). Place the 1 ×2 beneath the board along this line and drill three lead holes ¾ in. deep through the board into the base. Recess the screw heads. Glue and screw the base to the board (diagram b). Round off the lower edge of the base. Fill, sand, and paint the completed unit.

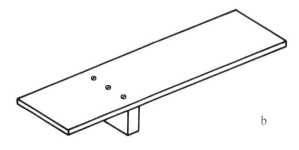

b

Variations

Construction
Frame the end of the board with quarter-round moulding or stripping to prevent a ball from rolling off the board (diagram c).

Place a yarn ball or bean bag on the end of the long arm of the board so that stamping on the short end propels the object into the air for catching or striking.

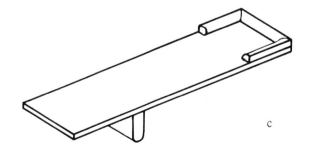

c

Batting tee

Supplies

Materials
wood—one 8 in. × 8 in. piece of ½ in. plywood
rubber plumber's plunger with handle
paint (optional)

Tools
drill, drill bit the same diameter as plunger handle, hand
saw, sandpaper, paintbrush

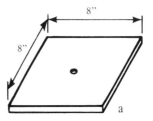

Construction

Drill a hole through the midpoint of the 8 in. × 8 in.
block (diagram a). Cut off the rounded end of the plunger
handle (diagram b) and insert the cut end into the hole in
the base (diagram c). Sand and paint unit.

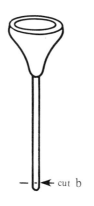
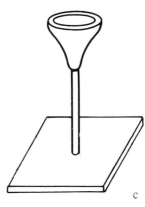

Variations

Materials
Select a plunger with a small opening for supporting small
balls.
Mount golf club tubes on a wooden dowel (diagram d). Ensure
a snug fit of the tube over the dowel.
Construction
Sharpen batting tee handles to stick into the ground for use out-
doors.
Size
Vary the height of the tees according to the needs of the chil-
dren using them.

The dowel and base unit used to support the golf club
tube batting tee can be used alone as a ring toss target.

Box and can targets

Supplies

Materials
milk cartons—any size
paper boxes—cereal, detergent, cracker, or similar
    types
cans—juice, coffee, or similar types
glue
masking tape
paint

Tools
scissors or a sharp knife, paintbrush

Construction

Milk cartons
Cut and fold the top of the carton so it lies flat. Remove any extra pieces and glue or tape the top in position. Decorate with enamel paint (diagram a).

Paper boxes
Tape the box openings flat. Paint all sides (diagram b).

Cans
Wash out cans and remove wrappers. Eliminate all sharp edges. Tape over holes or openings. Paint or cover with contact plastic (diagram c).

Variations

Materials
Use any material which can support canes or sticks.
Targets should be made of objects which can fall on contact and not damage floors.
Construction
Put sand or cement into supports needing more stability.
Size and shape
Vary the height, width, depth, and shape.

Use these objects as targets, goal-posts, boundary markers, or supports for a variety of canes, sticks, and dowels (see **Sticks**, p. 32).

a

b

c

Fixed can target

Supplies

Materials

cans—three 2 lb. coffee cans
wood—one 8 in. × 28 in. piece of ¾ in. plywood or
      hardwood
screws—six ½ in. screws
paint

Tools

drill, screwdriver, sandpaper, paintbrush

Construction

Drill two small holes in the bottom of each can. Paint the
cans. Prepare the board by sanding the rough edges and
surfaces and painting the desired colour. Space the cans
evenly along the board. Mark the positions of the holes.
Drill a hole ⅜ in. deep at each mark on the board. Screw
the cans firmly to the board (diagram a).

Variations

Materials

Use juice or fruit cans or the lower half of plastic bottles.

Construction

Paint the cans different colours for different scores.
Vary the positioning of the cans.
Use string instead of screws to secure the cans. *Note:* drill the
holes completely through the board. The cans can then be in-
terchanged.
Make a base for the board so it will stand up vertically (diagram b), or attach a string to one or both ends and hang it from
a hook or other support.

Size and shape

Use larger or variously sized cans.
Vary the shape of the base board to allow different positions of
the cans (diagram c).
Attach the sides of the cans to the front of the board so that the
can is parallel to the supporting board.

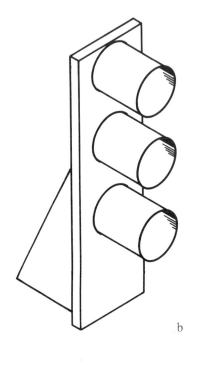

b

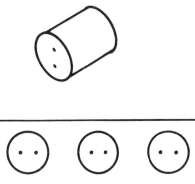

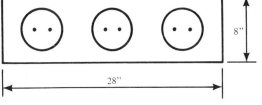

8"

28"

a

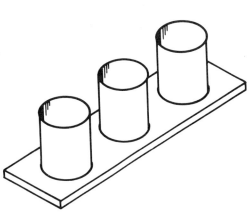

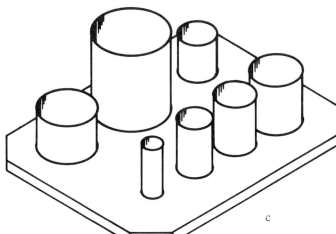

c

Solid block targets or supports

Supplies

Materials

wood—16 ft. of 4×4 (cedar or fir)
wood filler
lacquer, varnish, or paint

Tools

saw, sandpaper, electric or hand drill to drill a 1 in. diameter hole through 3½ in. of wood, putty knife, paintbrush

Construction

The 16 ft. length will yield the following: eight 12 in. blocks, eight 9 in. blocks, and four 6 in. blocks (diagram a). A 6 ft. piece of timber will yield two each of 6 in., 8 in., 10 in., and 12 in. blocks. Mark the proper hole and block locations on the 16 ft. length of 4 × 4 (diagram a). Position the holes 1¼ in. from the edge of the 4×4 and in the centre of each pair of blocks (diagram b). Drill 1 in. diameter holes. Saw each block off. Every second cut should bisect one of the drilled holes (diagram c). Fill and sand each block, making sure splinters, cracks, and flaws are repaired. The finish may be natural, stained, or painted.

Variations

Materials

Fir is stronger and less fragile than cedar; however, cedar is much lighter.
It is not necessary to start with a 16 ft. length of timber. Scraps can be used.

Size

The size may vary from the suggested dimensions, but three or four consistent sizes should be used rather than haphazard sizes. Keep in mind that these block supports tend to be unstable if they exceed 16 in. in height.

Use these blocks as targets, boundary markers, or goalposts as well as supports. The grooves make the blocks suitable for supporting cane or dowel **Sticks,** p. 32. The blocks will probably need to be quite durable and will require occasional refinishing.

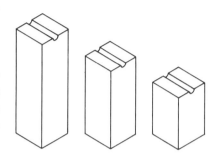

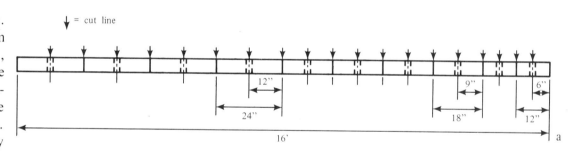

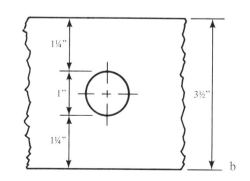

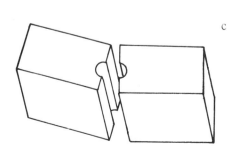

Flat target

Supplies

Materials
wood—one 2 ft. × 2 ft. piece of ⅜ in. plywood
wood filler
paint

Tools
saw, putty knife, sandpaper, paintbrush

Construction

Cut the wood to size. Fill flaws and holes, and sand. Mark and paint a design on the top surface of the target (diagram a).

Variations

Materials
Use plastic or linoleum scraps to cover the target or mark out targets.
Construction
To make a hanging target, cut holes as target areas and two holes for a rope loop (diagram b).
Size and shape
Vary target size, shape, markings, and colours (diagram c).

Bean bags or yarn balls will remain on the flat target after landing.

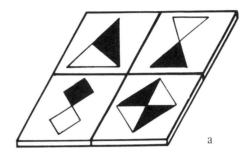

a

b

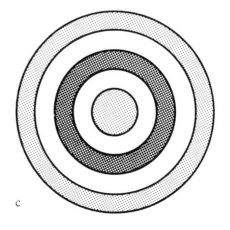

c

Standing shape target

Supplies

Materials

wood—left-over centre pieces from **Standing shape targets,** p. 25, or scrap lumber and plywood pieces (targets)

    —suitably sized pieces of ¾ in. plywood and 1×1 stripping (bases)

wood glue

wood filler

paint

Tools

sandpaper, putty knife, paintbrush

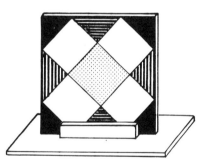

Construction

Targets

Fill, sand, and paint the target shapes.

Bases

Cut stripping pieces in half. Glue and nail these on the bases to form a groove that will hold the shape firmly.

Variations

Construction

Vary the designs or pictures on the targets as much as possible.

Size and shape

Change the size of the targets depending on the availability of materials and the distance at which they are to be used.

Vary the shape as well.

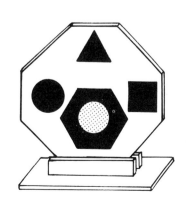

Peg targets

Supplies

Materials (basic single-peg target)

wood—one 15 in. × 15 in. piece of ¾ in. plywood
(base)

—10 in. length of old broom handle or ¾ in. dowel
(peg)

nails—one 1 in. nail

wood glue

paint

Tools

drill, ¾ in. bit (if dowel is used), hammer, sandpaper,
paintbrush

Construction

Locate the centre of the plywood piece by drawing lines
to opposite corners. Drill a ½ in. deep hole at the centre
and the same diameter as the handle or dowel. Glue the
handle or dowel in place and hammer the 1 in. nail into
the dowel through the plywood base (diagram a). Sand
all rough edges. Paint and decorate the completed unit
(diagram b).

Variations

Materials

Use a long, thin plastic bottle or a short stool leg instead of a
wooden peg.

Construction

Vary the number of pegs located on the base and their arrangement.

Nail the peg on from the back of the base if desired, eliminat-
ing the need to drill a hole.

Lean the targets against a wall or support them on tripods (dia-

grams c,d,e) so that **Rings,** p. 10, hang on the pegs rather than
land on the board.

By using a slant peg construction the same effect can be gained
with the board being vertical.

Vary the target designs.

Size and shape

Vary the size and shape of the base, as well as the height of the
pegs.

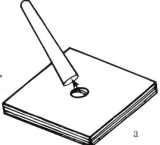

a

b

c

d

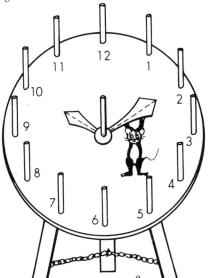

e

Cross peg target

Supplies

Materials

wood—one 3 ft. length of old broom handle or ¾ in. dowel (pegs)
—one 32 in. length of 1 ×4 hardwood board (base)
screws—¾ in. wood screws (or ¾ in. nails)
wood glue
wood filler
paint

Tools

hand saw, wood rasps, putty knife, drill, hammer (or screwdriver), sandpaper, paintbrush

Construction

Cut the dowel as follows: four 6½ in. lengths, one 10 in. length. Cut the hardwood in half. Mark the midline across each 16 in. piece, and measure 1¾ in. (half the width of the board) on either side of this line. Cut a notch across each board to a depth of ⅜ in. (diagram a). Rasp out and sand the notch and check the fit with the two base pieces. Attach the base pieces with the notches interlocking, using glue and small screws (do not put screws or nails in centre area of the overlapping pieces as a hole must be drilled at this point). Drill ¾ in. diameter holes to a depth of ½ in. at the four points 2 in. from each end and in the centre of the crossed pieces. Taper the top 1 in. of each peg. Glue the dowels into the drilled holes with the 10 in. dowel in the centre position (diagram b). Sand and paint.

Variations

Materials

Use old broom or mop handles instead of dowel for pegs.
Use left-over paint of various colours to make the unit more attractive.

Construction

The holes for the pegs can be drilled completely through and dowels glued in place.

Size

Vary the length of the base pieces or the pegs, or both.

Plan the board in conjunction with the rings to be used, because if the pegs are too close together rings may land over more than one peg.

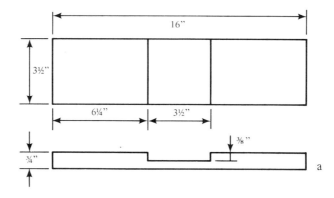

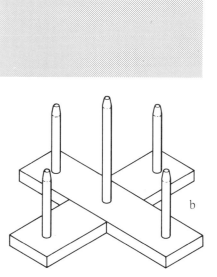

Hoop

Supplies

Materials
plastic tubing—8 ft. of ½ in. (inside diameter) tubing
wood—one 2 in. length of ½ in. dowel
glue
staples

Tools
sharp knife, staple gun

Construction

Cut the ends of the tubing at a slight angle so the outside edge, when held in a circle, will be slightly longer. Dip the ends of the wooden dowel into the glue and insert into the ends of the tube until the dowel is completely covered (diagram a). To fit the plug into the tube, place the ends of the tubing in hot water. The plastic will tighten on cooling. Secure the join by stapling the tubing to the plug (diagram b).

Variations

Materials
Use portions of discarded hoops as plugs.
Select different diameter tubing.

Vary the colour of the tubing.
Construction
Tape the join instead of stapling it.
Size
Vary the diameter of the hoop:

hoop diameter	tubing required
18 in.	4 ft. 9 in.
24 in.	6 ft. 3 in.
30 in.	7 ft. 10 in.
36 in.	9 ft. 6 in.
46 in.	12 ft. 6 in.

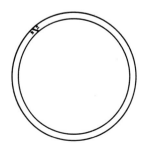

a   b

Hoop stands

Supplies

Materials

wood—one piece 5 in. × 15 in. of ¾ in. plywood or
    similar hardwood
hard cardboard
wood filler
paint

Tools

jig- and hand saw, drill, wood rasps, putty knife, sandpaper, paintbrush

Construction

Measure the diameter of the hoop tubing that is to be supported. Draw, on cardboard, the outline of the hoop
stand (diagram a). Cut out the cardboard pattern and use
it to trace two stands onto the plywood (diagram b). Cut
all straight edges, using a hand saw. With a drill bit
slightly smaller than the diameter of the hoop tube, to ensure a snug fit, drill a hole whose top edge is about ¼ in.
below the top border of the stand (diagram c). Cut
through to the hole, forming a groove for the hoop (diagram d), and rasp out the groove smoothly. Cut out the
arch with a jigsaw. Fill, sand, and paint the completed
stands. If the hoop is too loose, wrap it with tape where it
will sit in the grooves.

Variations

Materials

Vary the thickness of the plywood, but do not use less than
½ in. thick.

Size
Change the width and height of the stands according to the size
and weight of the hoop(s) to be supported. Very large hoops
need to have higher bases that are set farther apart.

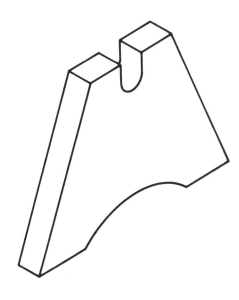

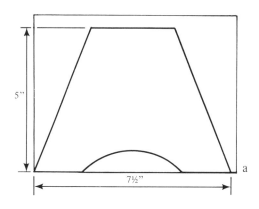

5"

7½"

a

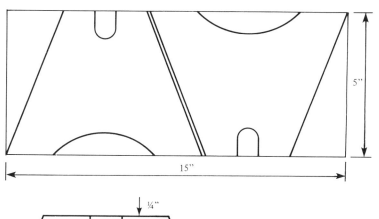

5"

15"

b

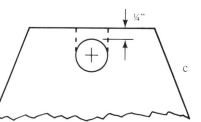

¼"

c

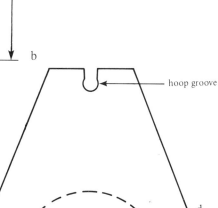

hoop groove

d

29

Standing shapes

Supplies

Materials

wood—one 4 ft. × 8 ft. sheet of ⅜ in. plywood (enough for two shape sets)

—¾ in. thick plywood and 1×1 finished stripping (use scraps and odd pieces for the smaller bases)

nails—1 in. finishing nails

wood glue

wood filler

paint

Tools

jig- or sabre saw, hammer, drill, putty knife, sandpaper, paintbrush

Construction

Shapes

Measure and draw shapes onto the sheet of plywood (diagram a). Draw circles, using a thin piece of wood stripping about 26 in. long with a drilled hole about 1 in. from the end. Measuring along the stick, drill holes 12¾ in., 15 in., 17½ in., 20½ in., and 24 in. from the first hole (diagram b). These holes should be large enough for a sharp pencil tip to protrude through. To draw a circle, tap a nail firmly through the guiding hole into the centre of the proposed circle set (diagram c). Hold a pencil in the last of the holes on the stick (24 in. from the guiding nail), then rotate until the circumference of the circle is complete. Move the pencil to the next hole and repeat until the whole set is drawn (diagram a). *Note:* always draw the largest size of each shape set first as this will guarantee enough wood inside the perimeter to complete that set. Cut out shapes using a jig-saw or sabre saw. Fill cracks or flaws, sand, and paint. The last is most easily done if shapes are hung on a suspended broom handle or pipe so that all sides can be painted at once.

Bases

A suggested size for bases holding the largest shapes is 18 in. × 6 in. Other bases may be smaller, depending on the size of the shapes to be supported. With glue and nails, attach two pieces of 1×1 spruce to the base to form a groove that will hold the shape firmly (diagram d). To prevent the circles from rolling out of their bases, saw or sand off a small part of the outside perimeter. This will provide a flat surface for the circles to rest on. Sand, fill, and paint the base.

Variations

Materials

Any material that can be supported by a small base and has enough strength to remain upright can be used for the shapes. Masonite may be adequate.

Construction

A minimum of wood is wasted when the shapes are cut concentrically. The left-over solid centres may be converted to other uses (see **Standing shape target,** p. 25).

Size and shape

Maximum size is limited by the nature of materials used.

Use virtually any shape, including triangles, squares, pentagons, rectangles, and octogons.

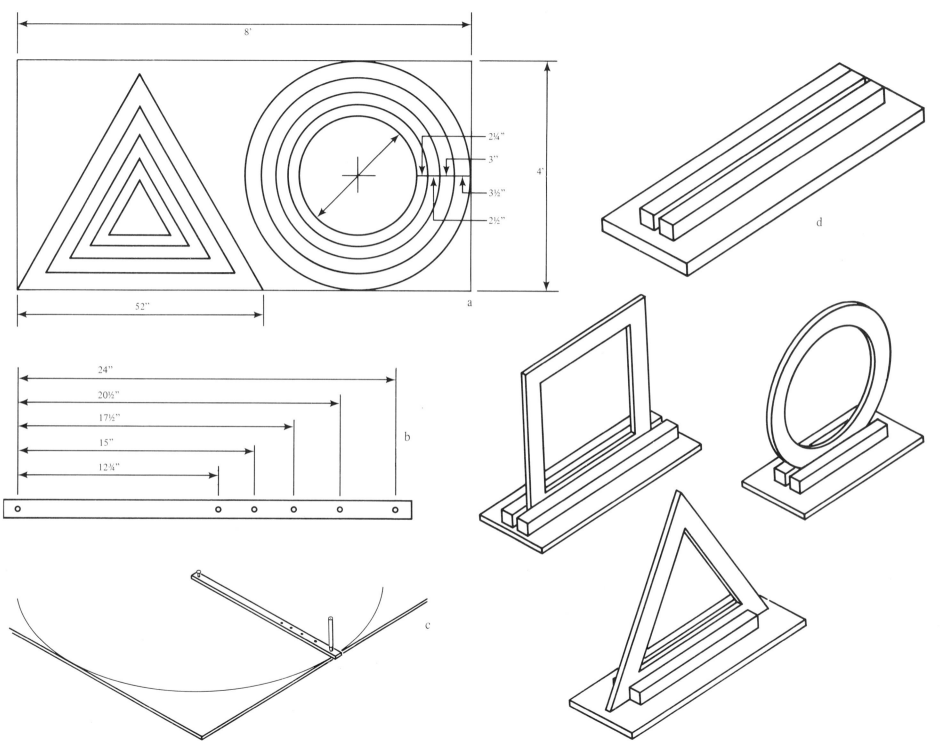

8'

2¼"

3"

3½"

2½"

4'

52"

a

d

24"

20½"

17½"

15"

12¾"

b

c

31

Sticks

Supplies

Materials
½ in. to ¾ in. diameter dowel
old broom handles
hockey sticks
half-round moulding
variously sized wood stripping
garden stakes or canes
shrub prunings
paint

Tools
hand saw, sandpaper, paintbrush

Construction

Cut the sticks to the desired length—3 ft. for short, up to 8 ft. for long ones. Sand all sticks. Paint various colours.

Variations

Materials
Use coloured tape to strengthen or decorate the sticks.
Size and shape
A wide variety of stick lengths is recommended.
It is useful to have some round sticks as well as square and flat ones.

The sticks should be compatible with the supports (see **Box and can targets,** p. 21, and **Solid block targets,** p. 23). Some supports are more suitable for round sticks, while flat-sided sticks will rest on most types of supports.

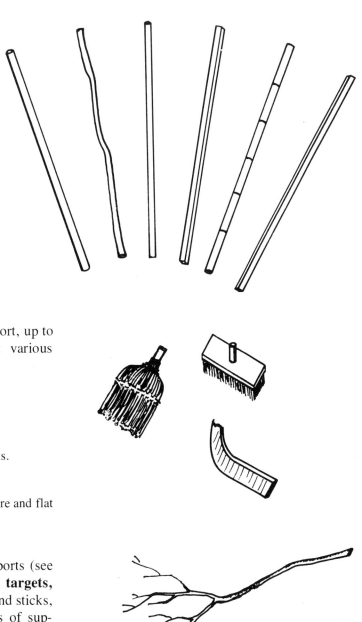

Solid cube

Supplies

Materials

wood—one 4 ft. × 5 ft. sheet of ⅜ in. finished
    plywood
    —about 18 ft. of 1×1 hardwood (bracing)
see **Cut-out cube,** p. 34, for remaining *Materials* and
Tools.

Construction

Follow same procedure as for Cut-out cube with the following differences:
top—18 in. × 17¼ in.; *base*—18 in. × 17¼ in.; *first
set of sides*—two 17¼ in. × 17¼ in.; *second set of
sides*—two 18 in. × 18 in. Cut a 1½ in. × 6 in. handle
slot out of the 18 in. × 18 in. side pieces. It is not necessary to paint or sand the interior. The relationship between the sides, top, and bottom is shown in diagram a.
The sides without handles fit inside the other pieces on
all edges. Attach the top last. Complete the bracing before this step. Sand the edges of the handles so they are
well rounded. Paint.

Variations

Materials
If wheeled casters are to be attached, the base must be thick
enough to provide solid attachment.
Construction
The cube can be made to accommodate the insertion of a plank
by adding bracing and enlarging the handle slot (diagram b).
The fit should be quite snug to provide stability. Such planks
should be supported at their free end so they are horizontal or
only slightly inclined.

Size
Vary the overall dimensions of the cubes.

The cubes should be planned so that they can be used ef-
fectively with other pieces of equipment. Therefore, co-
ordinated heights and dimensions will prove useful when
constructing other cubes, step sets, inclines, and similar
pieces.

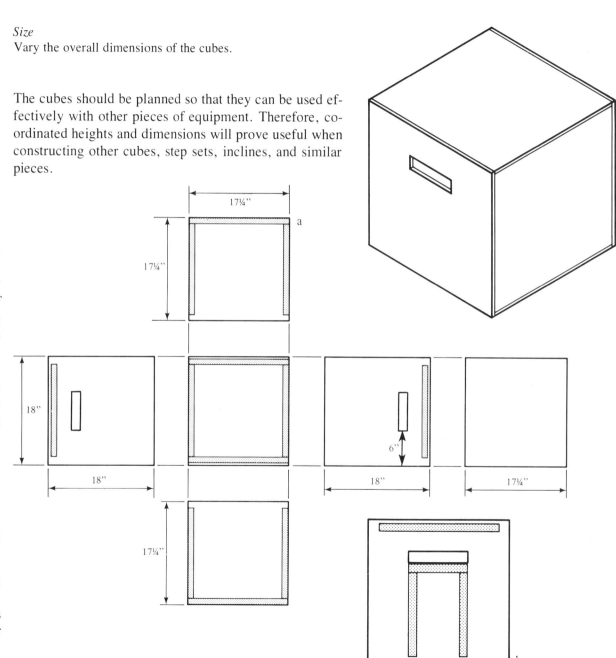

Cut-out cube

Supplies

Materials

wood—one 4 ft. × 6 ft. sheet of ⅜ in. finished
      plywood (cube)
      —about 24 ft. of 1 ×1 hardwood (bracing)
nails—1 in. finishing nails
wood glue
wood filler
paint

Tools

hand saw, jigsaw, sandpaper, hammer, putty knife,
paintbrush, wood clamps (optional)

Construction

Measure and cut the plywood for the cube as follows:
top—23¼ in. × 24 in.; *base*—24 in. × 24 in.; *first set
of opposite sides*—two 23¼ in. × 23¼ in.; *second set
of opposite sides*—two 24 in. × 23⅝ in.
Measure, draw, and cut out shapes in the four side pieces
(diagram a). A hand sabre saw or jigsaw may be necessary to cut out the variously shaped holes. Fill any cracks
and sand the cut out pieces. Attach bracing to the inside
of the side pieces (diagram b). Sand and paint the inside
surface and edges of all pieces. Attach the first set of opposite sides on to the base, using glue and nails (diagram
c). Attach the second set of opposite sides in the same
way (diagram d). Attach the top to the assembled
unit (diagram e). The top fits inside two ends and above
the other two opposite sides. Fill all flaws, sand
the outside, then paint. Finished dimensions are
24 in. × 24 in. × 24 in. *Note:* since the glue is the
major holding strength, tight, close fitting joints are es-
sential.

Variations

Construction

The side, base, and top arrangement may be varied. The top
could be above all four sides, but if the cube is to be used on its
sides every side needs some support.
Swivel casters may be attached to the base.

Size and shape

Vary the overall dimensions of the cube.
Vary the size, shape, and number of cutout sections; however,
at least one side should be solid to allow activity on top.

These units can be used in conjunction with step sets.
Use the left-over cutout pieces as targets, stepping
blocks, or boundary markers.

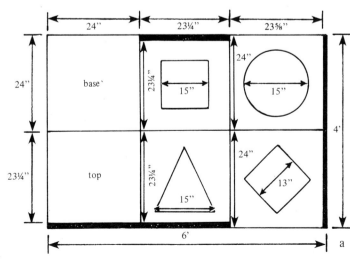

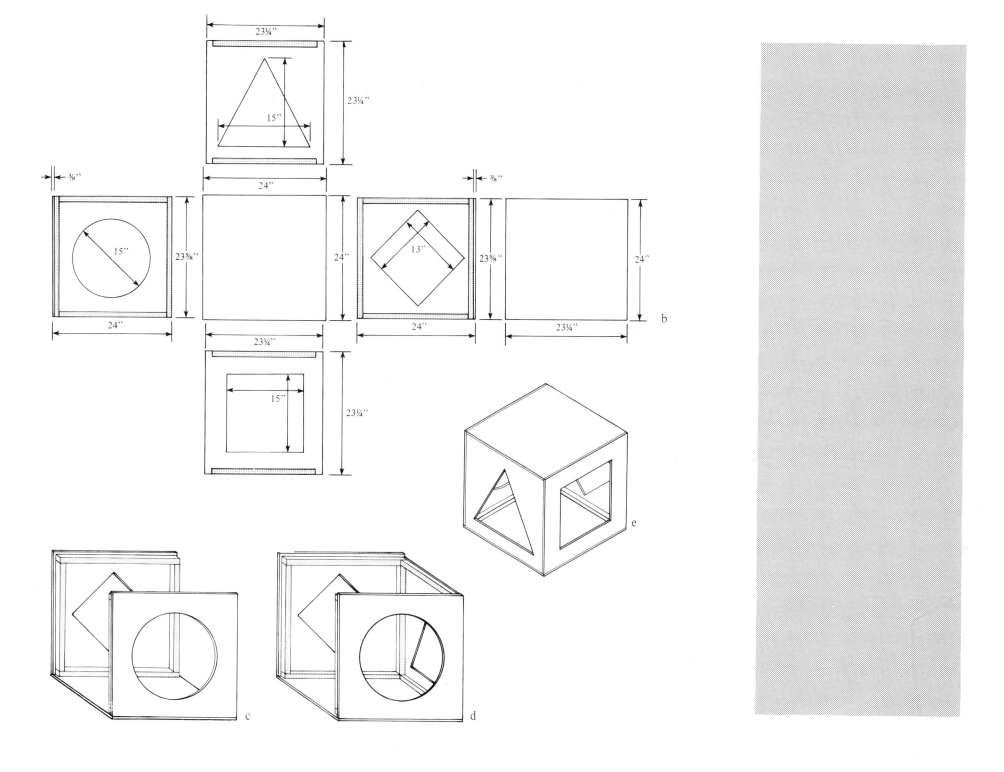

23¼"

23¼"

15"

24"

⅜"

15"

23⅝"

24"

24"

24"

⅜"

13"

23⅝"

24"

24"

23¼"

b

23¼"

15"

23¼"

e

c

d

35

Two-step unit

Supplies

Materials

wood—one 4 ft. × 5 ft. sheet of ⅜ in. finished plywood (if the side pieces have already been cut in conjunction with **Three-step unit,** p. 37, a 4 ft. × 4 ft. sheet will be adequate)
   —about 17 ft. of 1×1 hardwood
nails—1 in. finishing nails
wood glue
wood filler
paint

Tools

hand saw, sabre or coping saw, hammer, putty knife, sandpaper, paintbrush, clamps (optional)

Construction

Measure and cut pieces as follows:
back—24 in. × 15⅝ in.; *base*—23¼ in. × 15¼ in. (optional); *sides*—two (diagram a); *1st step*—24 in. × 8⅜ in.; *top step*—24 in. × 8 in.; *risers*—two 24 in. × 7⅝ in.

The step and riser relationship is shown in diagram b. Cut handle slots in the side pieces (diagram a). Cut and attach the 1×1 bracing to the side pieces with glue and nails, placing each piece flush with the edges (diagram a). Attach the back to the sides. If base is used, add necessary bracing. Attach the steps and risers, beginning with the bottom riser. This provides support for the step above. Glue and nail all joints. Fill flaws on the outside with wood filler. Sand all surfaces smooth, including the handle slots. Paint. Final dimensions are 16 in. × 16 in. × 24 in. (diagram b).

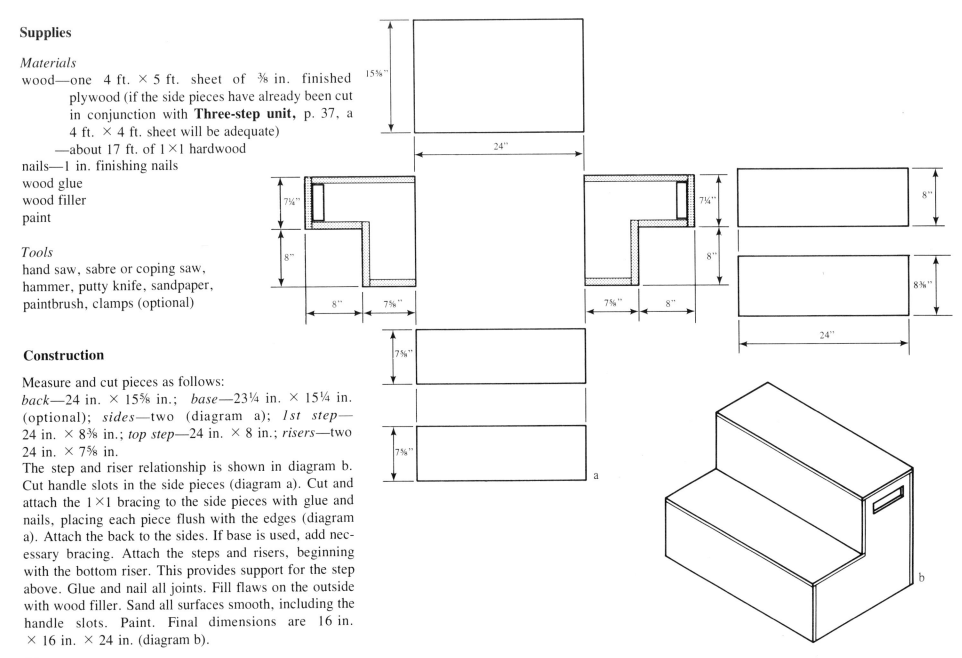

36

Three-step unit A

Supplies

Materials

wood—one 4 ft. × 6 ft. sheet of ⅜ in. finished
  plywood (if the two side pieces have already
  been cut, a piece 4 ft. × 4 ft. is sufficient)
  —about 18 ft. of 1×1 hardwood (bracing)
other *Materials* and *Tools* as for **Two-step unit,** p. 36

Construction

Measure and cut pieces as follows:
back—24 in. × 17¼ in.; *base*—24 in. × 18 in.;
sides—two (diagram b); *1st and 2nd steps*—two
24 in. × 6⅜ in.; *top step*—24 in. × 6 in.; *1st riser*—
24 in. × 5¼ in.; *other risers*—two 24 in. × 5⅝ in.
Follow the same assembly instructions as for the Two-
step unit. The step and riser relationship is shown in diagram a. The assembled unit is 18 in. high × 24 in. wide
(diagram c).

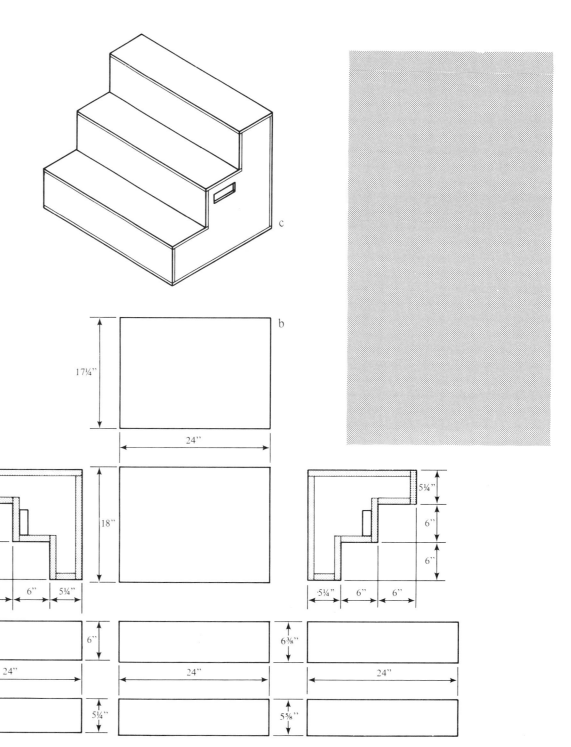

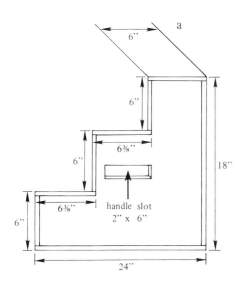

Three-step unit B

Supplies

Materials

wood—one 4 ft. × 6 ft. sheet of ⅜ in. finished
plywood (this will allow the side pieces to be cut
in conjunction with the Two-step unit)
—about 22 ft. of 1 × 1 hardwood (bracing)
other *Materials* and *Tools* as for **Two-step unit,** p. 36

Construction

Measure and cut pieces as follows:
back—24 in. × 23¼ in.; *base*—24 in. × 24 in.;
sides—two (diagram a); *1st and 2nd steps*—two
24 in. × 8⅜ in.; *top step*—24 in. × 8 in.; *1st riser*—
24 in. × 7¼ in.; *2nd and 3rd risers*—two
24 in. × 7⅝ in.
Follow the same assembly instructions as for the Two-
step unit. Final dimensions are 24 in. × 24 in. × 24 in.
Note: the circle in the back is 15 in. in diameter. The step
and riser relationship and bracing scheme are shown in
diagrams b, c.

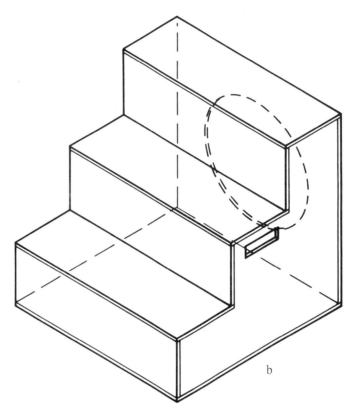

b

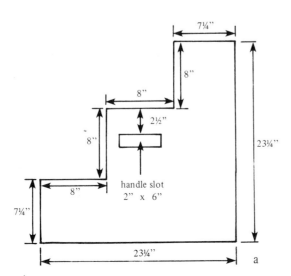

a

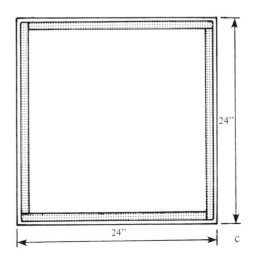

c

Four-step unit

Supplies

Materials

wood—one 4 ft. × 8 ft. sheet of ⅜ in. finished plywood

nails—1 in. finishing nails

other *Materials* and *Tools* as for **Two-step unit,** p. 36

Construction

The side pieces may be planned and cut in conjunction with the sides for the Three-step unit B (diagram a). Measure and cut pieces as follows:

back—24 in. × 23¼ in.; *base*—24 in. × 24 in.; *sides*—two (diagram a); *top step*—24 in. × 6 in.; *first three steps*—three 24 in. × 6⅜ in.; *1st riser*—24 in. × 5¼ in.; *three remaining risers*—three 24 in. × 5⅝ in.

Follow the same assembly instructions as for the Two-step unit.

Variations

Materials

Increase the thickness of the wood according to the age and size of the children using the equipment.

Construction

Metal bracing on the underside of the step and riser connections will provide extra support. If this is used, attach the base last.

Size

Consider the following size variations to adapt the units to the children using them: step depth, riser height, number of steps, and unit width. If the unit is large enough, cut a hole in the back to provide an enclosed space under the steps.

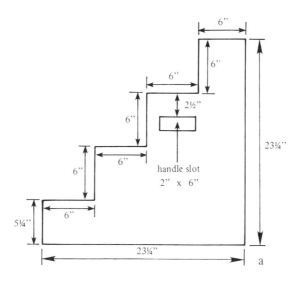

handle slot
2" x 6"

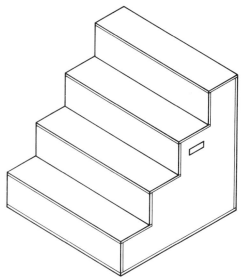

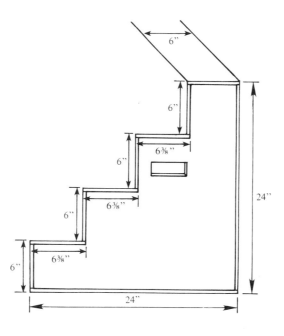

5 A frames

Sawhorse

Supplies

Materials
wood—12 ft of 2×4 hardwood
 —22 in. × 5 in. piece of ¾ in. plywood
nails—2½ in. long
wood glue
wood filler
paint

Tools
hand saw, wood rasp, chisel, clamps (optional), hammer, putty knife, sandpaper, paintbrush

Construction

From the 2×4 cut the following pieces:
legs—four 24 in. each; *top*—one 46 in.
Saw, chisel, and rasp grooves in the top bar for the legs. These grooves begin 6½ in. from the end, are 3½ in. long, and ½ in. deep at the top (diagram a). *Note:* if the angle of the legs is changed, the angle of the grooves must be altered correspondingly. Hold a leg in place in the groove and measure the triangle to be cut off to make it flush with the top of the bar (diagram a). Trim the legs. Using glue and nails, attach one pair of legs to the bar.

While the glue sets, measure each plywood brace for the top of the legs and cut (diagram b). Repeat with the second pair of legs (diagram c). Fill flaws, sand thoroughly, and paint (diagram d).

Variations

Materials
Use any thickness or type of wood for the braces which will withstand stress, or use commercial sawhorse clamps instead of constructing the horse as outlined.
Construction
Use screws instead of nails for added durability.
Rubber strips on the feet of the sawhorse will protect floors.
Size and shape
The sawhorse may be longer, taller, or have a wider base. The dimensions may also be scaled down to suit other purposes.

The sawhorse may be used as a plank support, balance apparatus, or crawl-through frame. Special functions may require the addition of special slots or accessories.

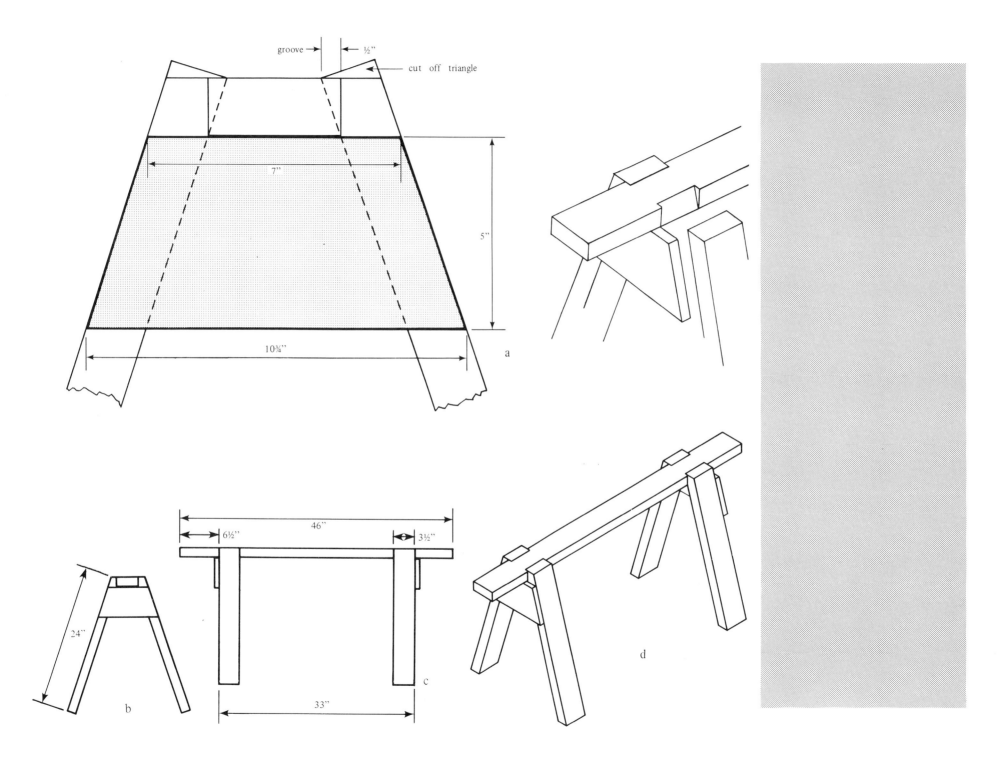

groove

½"

cut off triangle

7"

5"

10¾"

a

46"

6½"

3½"

24"

b

33"

c

d

41

Trestles

Supplies

Materials

The following will yield three trestles:

wood—one 4 ft. × 6½ ft. sheet of 1 in. plywood (triangle frames)

—one 4 ft. × 8 ft. sheet of ¾ in. plywood (platforms)

—seventeen 1 in. diameter hardwood dowels each 32 in. long (choose dowel with the grain parallel to long axis)

—16 ft. of 2×2 spruce (or 1 in. plywood scraps)

nails—1½ in. long

wood glue

wood filler

paint

Tools

hand saw, jig- or sabre saw, drill with 1 in. bit, hammer, putty knife, sandpaper, paintbrush

Construction

Triangle frames

Measure, mark, and cut the large triangular shapes from the 1 in. plywood (diagram a). Cut the smaller triangle frames from the two large ones, using a jigsaw or sabre saw. This will yield three pairs of triangles, each pair being a different size (diagram b). Drill 1 in. diameter holes through the frames (diagram c). Cut the 2×2 bracing to yield: two 45 in. long for large triangle, two 33 in. long for medium triangle, and two 21 in. long for small triangle. Using glue and nails, attach the platform bracing (diagram c). The braces should be flush to the floor so they can help support the trestle's weight. Fill flaws, then sand smooth.

Platforms

Using the ¾ in. plywood, mark and cut the platforms (diagram d). Fill and sand smooth.

Dowel bars

Cut the dowels to yield seventeen bars, each 32 in. in length. Sand smooth. Check the fit of the dowels into the drilled holes.

Assembly

Attach the large platform (30 in. × 45 in.) to the pair of large triangular frames by gluing and nailing the platform to the 2×2 braces (diagram e). Before unit is set, apply glue to the dowels near the ends and insert into the drilled holes so that dowel ends are flush with the outside of the triangular frames. Insert the dowels from the bottom upwards. Allow the glue to dry completely and then fill flaws. Sand and paint. Follow the same procedure with the second and third pair of triangular frames.

Construction

The 2×2 bracing can be replaced by scraps from the 1 in. sheet of plywood. A certain amount of variation in the lengths of the braces is acceptable.

If each smaller trestle is made with shorter dowels and the platforms eliminated, the trestles will stack for storage.

Size and shape

The shape of the trestle could be square or rectangular, but the advantages of a stable A frame would be lost.

Variations

The size of the units should vary according to the age of the children using the equipment, the space available, and the materials obtainable. The 30 in. span suggested here can be increased or decreased; however, a longer span allows more bend and gives less support to the bars. The width of the planks used with this apparatus will, in part, determine the minimal span between frames because two planks should be able to be accommodated side by side in some arrangements. Thus a 12 in. wide plank requires at least a 24 in. dowel span. Since the dowels are inserted into the frames, they must be cut 2 in. longer than the span.

Plan cleated planks in conjunction with this platform trestle set so that the various pieces complement each other.
Platforms may be omitted; however, they add strength and provide a crawl space.

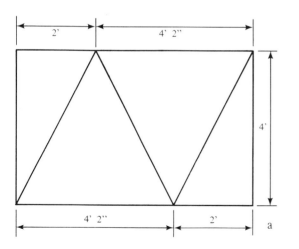

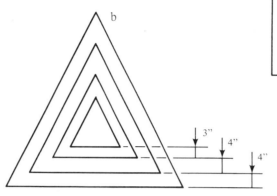

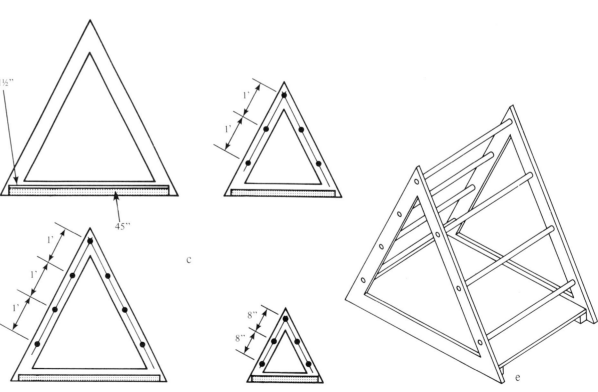

6 Stationary balance structures

Stepping blocks

Supplies

Materials
wood—left-over pieces of varying width, length, and
     thickness
rubber—foam or old carpet underlay (rubber type)
wood glue
wood filler
paint or varnish

Tools
hand or coping saw, putty knife, sandpaper, paintbrush,
scissors

Construction

Draw chosen shapes on wood scraps (diagram a) and cut
out. To make a thick block, glue several identically
shaped pieces together (diagram b). Fill all cracks and
flaws and sand blocks thoroughly, rounding off any
sharp corners. Varnish or paint. When dry, glue rubber
or foam backing to the block base to prevent slipping.

Variations

Materials
Almost any kind of wood may be used, but very soft, splintery

kinds should be avoided.
Construction
If only thin wood scraps are available, use many-layered la-
minations.
Size
The blocks can be of almost any dimensions, but the minimum
diameter should be 3 in.
As the height increases, so should the diameter to ensure sta-
bility.

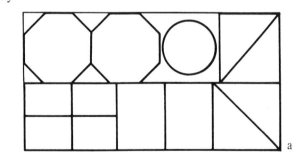
a

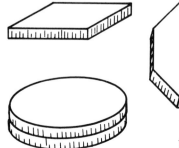
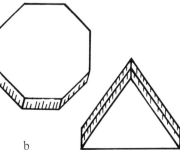
b

Balance rail

Supplies

Materials
wood—18 in. × 16 in. × ¾ in. finished plywood
    (base)
    —18 in. of 2×2 spruce or fir (rail)
nails—1¼ in. long
wood glue
wood filler
paint

Tools
saw, hammer, putty knife, sandpaper, paintbrush

Construction

Cut the plywood to 18 in. × 16 in. Cut one 18 in.
length of 2×2. Using glue and nails, attach the rail to the
midline of the plywood base (diagram a). Fill cracks and
flaws, sand, and paint.

Variations

Construction
Use screws instead of nails for greater strength.
Size
Larger bases could be used but generally should not be neces-
sary. Vary the rail height and width, however, to provide a
wider range of balance challenges (diagram b).

Balance rails of the type outlined here are used for static
balance activities but can be constructed so that, when in-
verted, the rail becomes a balance board.

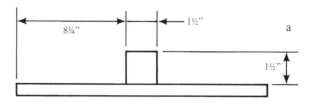

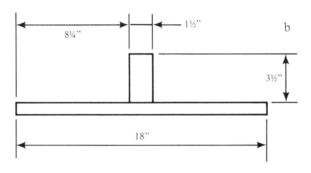

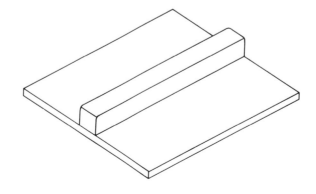

Balance beam and bases

Supplies

Materials
wood—8 ft. of 2×4 hardwood (beam)
    —2 ft. of 2×4 hardwood (base)
    —16 in. × 1 in. of 1 in. thick plywood (base)
nails—1¾ in. and 3 in. lengths
wood glue
wood filler
varnish or paint

Tools
hand saw, hammer, putty knife, sandpaper, paintbrush

Construction

Sand all edges and paint or varnish the 8 ft. beam. Construct the base by cutting the short 2×4 into six 4 in. pieces. Join the three pieces together as shown (diagram a). Glue and nail in position. Cut the plywood strip into four equal lengths. Place two of these on top of the horizontal 2×4 and against the vertical side pieces (diagram b). Glue and nail into position. Fill, sand, and paint or varnish. Position the beam either horizontally or vertically (diagram c).

Variations

Construction
Use screws instead of nails, but the heads must be recessed and filled.
Size
Vary the length, height, and width of the balance beam set. If the length is over 8 ft. a third base may be needed at the midpoint of the beam.

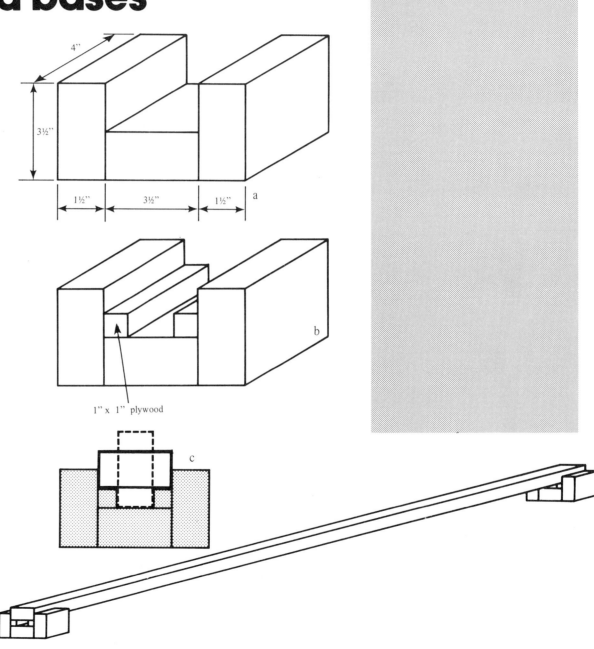

Balance beam and one-piece bases

Supplies

Materials

wood—one 6½ ft. length of 2×4 hardwood (beam)
　　—one 13 in. length of 2×4 hardwood (bases)
wood filler
paint or varnish

Tools

saw, rasp, putty knife, sandpaper, paintbrush

Construction

Sand and paint the longer 2×4. Cut the other 2×4 into two 6½ in. pieces. On each base piece cut a notch 3½ in. wide × 1½ in. deep, and 1½ in. in from each end. Cut a second notch 1½ in. wide × 1 in. deeper than the base of the first notch (diagram a). This smaller notch should be centred 1 in. from each edge of the first notch. Now the beam can be used on either face. Rasp and sand the notches and base pieces smooth. Paint or varnish.

Variations

Materials

Use heavier wood for the bases and beam, such as 2×6 instead of 2×4.

Construction

If the beam is longer than 8 ft., a middle base should be used. For more stability, nail a 6 in. × 8 in. platform made of ¾ in. plywood onto the base (diagram b).

Size

Vary the length of the beam as well as the height of the beam above the floor.

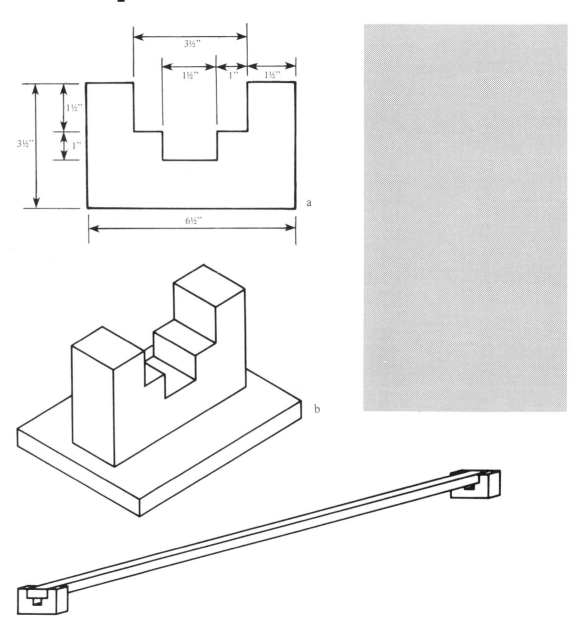

Upright base balance board

Supplies

Materials
wood—one 16 in. × 16 in. piece of ¾ in. plywood
    (balance board)
    —one 16 in. length of 2×3 hardwood (base)
screws—three 1½ in. wood screws
wood glue
wood filler
paint

Tools
hand saw, rasp, sandpaper, drill, screwdriver, putty
knife, paintbrush

Construction

Rasp and sand the 2×3 along one edge to make a
rounded surface. Mark a line bisecting the plywood
board, centre the base on this line, and attach with glue
and screws through the plywood (diagram a). Recess the
screw heads. Fill all holes and cracks, sand smooth, and
paint.

Variations

Materials
Vary the thickness of the platform board.
Construction
Attach a non-slip material to the top surface of the plywood
platform.
Leave the floor edge of the base square.
Size
Vary the dimensions of the platform, as well as the height and
width of the base.

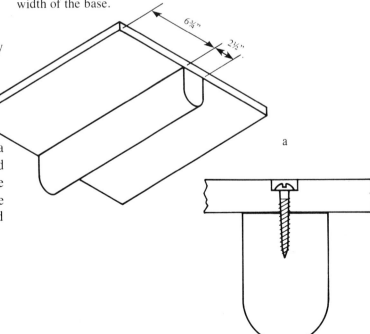

a

Pivot base balance board

Supplies

Materials

wood—one 12 in. × 18 in. piece of ¾ in. plywood (balance board)
    —one 1 ft. length of 2 × 3 hardwood (base)
bolt—one ¼ in. carriage bolt 2½ in. long, plus nut and two washers
wood filler
paint

Tools

hand saw, putty knife, sandpaper, drill, paintbrush, centre punch

Construction

Fill and sand board and base. Drill a ¼ in. diameter hole through the centre of the plywood and hardwood. Recess the nut joining the board to the balance piece by drilling a ½ in. diameter hole in the centre of the plywood to a depth of about ⅛ in. (diagram a). Make a deep recess, 1 in. in diameter and 1 in. deep, in the bottom of the 2 × 3 base piece to house the nut of the bolt (diagram a). Paint both pieces of the unit. Insert the carriage bolt through the hole in the large board and then through the base. Slip two washers onto the bolt, screw on the nut, and tighten. Set the nut with a centre punch to ensure that it cannot fall off. The angle of the base should be changed to provide a variety of balance situations. To do this, loosen the nut, rotate the base, then tighten the nut again.

Variations

Size and shape

Vary the thickness of the plywood or the base dimensions. Vary the size and shape of the platform. Larger platforms need correspondingly higher bases. Make the platform oval, square, hexagonal, or some other shape.

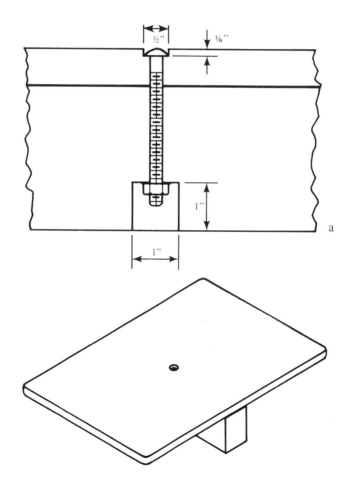

a

Square base balance board

Supplies

Materials

wood—one 16 in. × 16 in. piece of ¾ in. plywood
    (balance board)
      —one 3½ in. length of 4×4 (base)
screws—four 1½ in. wood screws
wood glue
wood filler
paint

Tools

saw, sandpaper, drill, screwdriver, putty knife, paintbrush

Construction

Sand and smooth the base cube. Mark the centre of the
plywood board and centre the base cube on this point
(diagram a). Drill small lead holes for the four wood
screws, as well as shallow depressions to recess the
screw heads. Using glue and screws, attach the plywood
platform to the cube base (diagram b). Fill, sand, and
paint.

Variations

Construction
Round off the bottom corners of the base cube.
Two 2×4s may replace the 4×4. In this case they should be
glued together first to make a cube.
Size and shape
Vary the thickness of the wood, the size and shape of the plat-
form, and the height of the base.

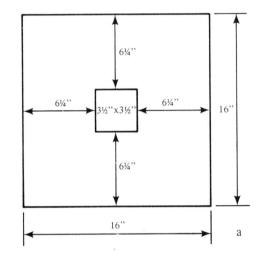

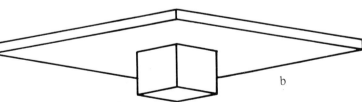

50

Curved base balance board

Supplies

Materials

wood—one 18 in. × 18 in. piece of ¾ in. plywood (balance board)
—two 18 in. pieces of 1 ×3 hardwood (base)
screws—eight 1½ in. wood screws
nails—1¼ in. finishing nail
wood glue
wood filler
paint

Tools

hand saw, jig- or sabre saw, rasps, screwdriver, hammer, putty knife, sandpaper, paintbrush

Construction

Draw an 18 in. diameter circle on the ¾ in. plywood (diagram a). Using a jigsaw or sabre saw, cut out the circle. Fill any flaws in the wood and sand the circle smooth. Draw a curved edge on each of the two hardwood pieces. The maximum height of the arc of this curve is 2½ in. and must be located at the midpoint of the board (diagram b). Cut out these pieces with a jigsaw or sabre saw. Cut notches as indicated, 1½ in. deep and ¾ in. wide. *Note:* the notch is on the straight edge of one piece and on the curved edge of the other (diagram c). Use the rasp to clean out the notches. Place the two hardwood pieces together, interlocking the notches, and glue securely (diagram d). Hammer in a finishing nail from the top piece. Place the plywood circle on the flat side of the rocker base and attach with glue and screws from the top. Recess the screw heads, fill and sand all surfaces smooth, and paint.

Variations

Construction

Use a ring in place of the solid platform. The ring is 18 in. in diameter and 3 in. wide (diagram e).

Size and shape

Vary the diameter of the solid or ring platforms, which may be greater than 18 in. as well as less.
Vary the base height.
Change the shape of the platform.

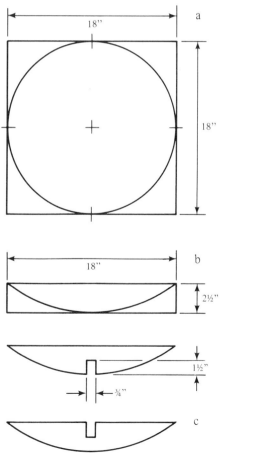

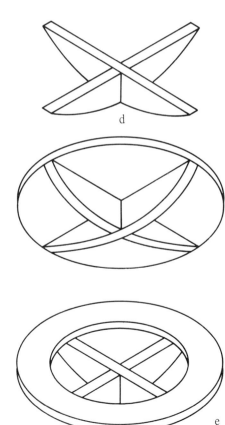

Pyramid base balance board

Supplies

Materials

wood—one 17¼ in. × 20 in. piece of ¾ in. plywood
    —three 12 in. lengths of 1×3 hardwood (base)
screws—nine 1½ in. wood screws
wood glue
wood filler
paint

Tools

saw, protractor, drill, screwdriver, putty knife, sandpaper, paintbrush

Construction

Cut an equilateral triangle from the plywood (diagram a). Using a protractor to bisect each 60 degree corner angle, locate the centre of the triangle (diagram b). Alternatively, the angles may be bisected by drawing a line from each point to the midpoint of the opposite side. Draw a line from the centre to each corner. Place one of the 12 in. lengths of hardwood along one of these lines to check the fit. Cut if necessary. Measure 2 in. from one end of each hardwood piece and cut from that point diagonally to a point at the other end (diagram c). Place all three pieces of hardwood along the lines on the triangle so that they meet at the centre. Rasp and sand to ensure a good fit (diagram d). Drill lead holes for three screws along each hardwood piece. Holes should be drilled through the platform into the hardwood since this is the direction in which the screws will be driven. Round off the corners of triangle and, with glue and screws, attach it to the hardwood pieces (diagram e). Fill cracks and holes, sand, and paint.

Variations

Construction

Round off the sides of the triangle.

Size

Vary the size and height of the unit, also the wood thickness.

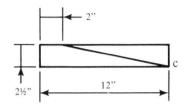

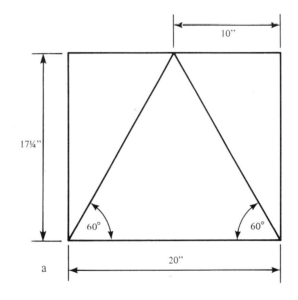

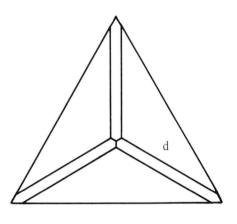

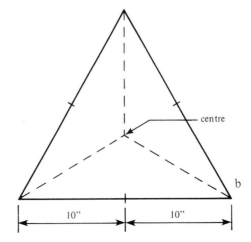

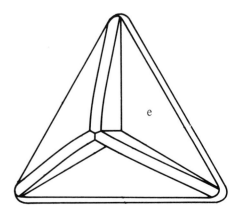

Beam base balance

Supplies

Materials
wood—one 20 in. length of 2×3 hardwood
screws—two 2½ in. wood screws
wood glue
wood filler
paint

Tools
saw, screwdriver, rasps, drill, putty knife, sandpaper, paintbrush

Construction

Cut the 2×3 into one 14 in. piece and one 6 in. piece. Locate the midpoint of each piece and centre a notch at this point (diagram a). Make the notch 1½ in. wide and ¾ in. deep. Check before cutting to ensure it is wide enough to accommodate the other piece of wood (diagram b). Rasp out the cut notches. Join pieces together with notches interlocking, and glue (diagram c). Drill lead holes for the screws, recess and fill heads. Fill flaws, sand, and paint.

Variations

Construction
Round off the support beam to protect floors.
Size
Vary the length of the beam and the height of the base.

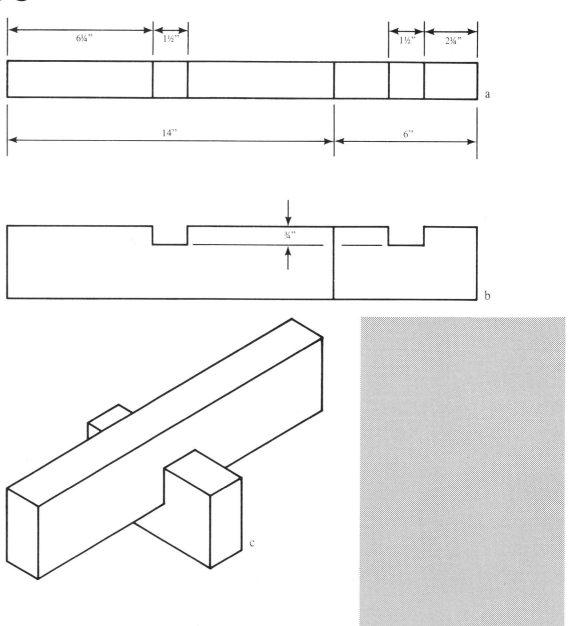

Balance plank

Supplies

Materials

wood—one 6 ft. × 8 in. piece of ¾ in. finished
      plywood or hardwood (plank)
     —one 6 ft. length of 2 ×2 spruce (base)
screws—approximately 1½ in. wood screws
wood glue
wood filler
paint

Tools

saw, drill with ¼ in. bit, screwdriver, putty knife, sandpaper, paintbrush

Construction

Cut the plywood to size and align the 2×2 along centre
line of the plank (diagrams a,c). Attach the plank to the
base with glue and wood screws spaced approximately
8 in. apart (diagram b). Fill the recessed screw heads.
Sand smooth and round all edges (sanding may also be
done as each piece is finished), then paint.

Variations

Size

Vary the plank thickness from ½ in. to 1 in.
Vary the width and length of the plank. A very wide plank,
however, will need a larger base or there will be very little tipping possible before the edge of the plank touches the floor.

The plank should be long enough for walking its length.
Too short a plank simply becomes a balance board. The
completed apparatus can be used, when turned over, as a
narrow beam with a wide stable base. This requires careful sanding and filling of the support board for use with
bare feet.

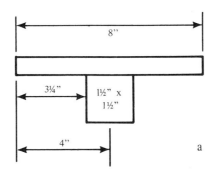

a

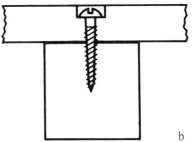

b

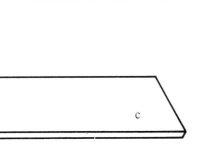

c

Curved base rocker board

Supplies

Materials

wood—one 12 in. × 18 in. piece of ¾ in. plywood
  (platform)
  —one 36 in. length of 1 ×4 hardwood (base)
screws—approximately eight 1½ in. wood screws
wood glue
wood filler
paint

Tools

hand saw, jig- or sabre saw, screwdriver, drill, putty
knife, sandpaper, paintbrush

Construction

Cut the 1 ×4 hardwood into two 18 in. lengths (diagram
a). Mark and cut out a rocker from one of the hardwood
pieces (diagram b). The curved line can be made by
using a circular object that will cut through both corners
on one side and reach the midpoint of the opposite side at
the peak of the arc. Use the edge of a hoop or tie a pencil
to a string and hold the string at various positions below
the board until the needed curve is obtained. Use the first
rocker to trace out the second. Make sure flat edges are
flush. Cut out second rocker. Fill and sand both rockers,
making certain they remain identical. Drill lead holes for
the screws in both platform and rockers. Attach the platform to rockers using glue and screws (diagram c). Recess screw heads. Fill flaws in wood, sand,
and paint.

Variations

Materials

Fasten various padding or non-slip materials to the platform.

Construction

In the above version the rockers are along the length of the
board. The rockers can also be crossways on the platform,
making rocking more difficult.

A brace may be added which extends across the platform between the rockers. This should be a 16½ in. piece of 2 ×2 for
the rocker described.

Size

Vary the size of the platform, as well as the height of the
rocker, by using different sizes of hardwood, such as 1 ×6 instead of 1 ×4.

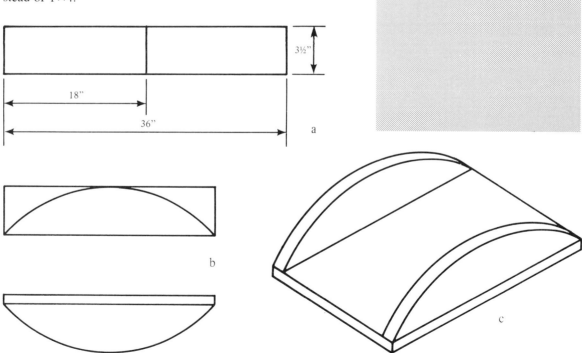

3½"

18"

36"

a

b

c

Roller board

Supplies

Materials

wood—one 18 in. × 14 in. piece of ¾ in. plywood (board)
—one 28 in. length of 1 ×1 hardwood (cleats)
screws—four 1 in. wood screws
heavy cardboard roll 3 to 6 in. diameter and 16 in. long (roller)
wood glue
wood filler
masking tape
paint

Tools

saw, drill, screwdriver, putty knife, sandpaper, paintbrush

Construction

Draw two lines, each 6 in. from the edge and parallel to the 14 in. sides of the plywood. Cut the hardwood in half and, using glue and screws, attach the two 14 in. pieces to the plywood along the lines just marked (diagram a). Fill flaws. Reinforce the ends of the cardboard roll with masking tape to prevent unravelling. Sand and paint the total unit (diagram b).

Variations

Construction
Vary the distance between the hardwood cleats, making it less for beginners.
Size and shape
Vary the size and thickness of the board to suit the children using it. Narrower and longer versions are recommended as further variations.
Vary the diameter of the roller.

Rollers of the type required are often available from carpet dealers or floor covering suppliers.

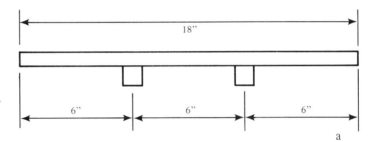

a

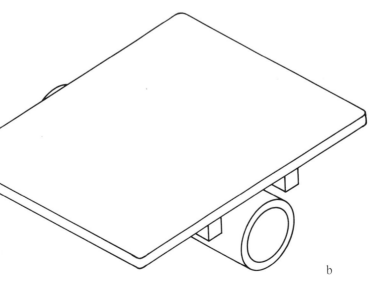

b

Scooter board

Supplies

Materials

wood—one 12 in. × 12 in. piece of ¾ in. plywood (platform)
wheels—four mounted swivel casters
screws—sixteen ½ to ¾ in. wood screws (for casters)
wood filler
paint
tape—48 in. length of ¾ in. wide plastic tape

Tools

saw, rasp, drill, screwdriver, putty knife, sandpaper, paintbrush

Construction

Round off the corners of the platform. Fill flaws and sand, then paint the board. Using casters to mark the screw locations, drill small lead holes. Screw the casters in place (diagrams a,b). Tape around the edge of the scooter board.

Variations

Construction

Use an old, small bicycle tire around the edge of a circular scooter to protect walls and the scooter edge, securing it with screws and washers.
To store scooters so they stay together but take up little space, attach a removable post to one scooter and slide the other scooters down the post to form a vertical stack. To do this attach a floor flange to the underside of one scooter and place a pipe or dowel through a drilled hole in scooter board firmly into the floor flange (diagram c). All scooters with a central hole drilled in them can now be stored on this pole.

Cover scooters with carpet underlay or carpet glued in place.

Size and shape

Vary the size of the scooter and thickness of the board to suit the children using it.
The scooters can be made in almost any shape (diagram d), but a triangular one requires only three casters.

Keep casters well lubricated.

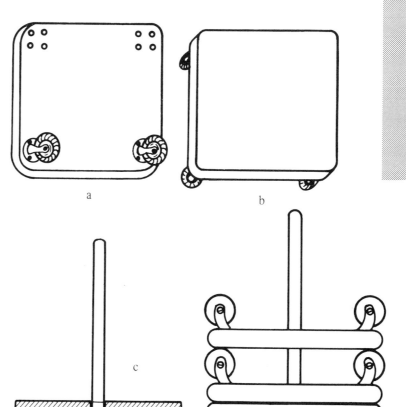

a

b

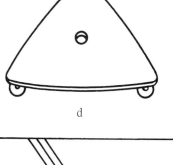

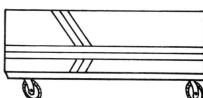

c

d

8 Horizontal and inclined structures

Planks

Supplies

Materials
wood—various sizes of ¾ in. plywood or hardwood
   (planks)
   —various lengths of 2×2 hardwood (cleats)
nails—1 in. finishing nails or screws
wood glue
wood filler
paint

Tools
saw, hammer, putty knife, sandpaper, paintbrush

Construction

Cut planks to the lengths and widths desired. These will depend on the nature of the equipment with which these planks are to be used and the space available. Cut the 2×2 so that for every support point there are two cleats across the full width of the plank. Glue and nail the cleats to the planks (diagram a). The spacing between these cleats will depend on the thickness of the bar or board which must fit between them. Fill all flaws, sand smooth, and paint (diagram b).

Variations

Materials
Use metal hooks for the tops of inclined planks instead of the 2×2 cleats. These hooks should be covered with leather or rubber to prevent their "chewing" and damaging other equipment. If hooks are to be used, thicker wood (1 in.) is necessary so they can be screwed to the wood.

Construction
If the plank is to extend from one piece of equipment to another, cleats should be at both ends of the board for stability and safety. A third set of cleats may be added at the midpoint of the plank as an additional support point for long planks. If the plank is strong enough, the middle groove could also be the pivotal point for a teeter-totter.

The planks can be padded with a layer of foam or carpet underlay and covered by vinyl or leather stapled or tacked to the underside.

Size
Planks of a variety of widths and lengths should be made.

These planks are very useful in conjunction with bar boxes, metal A frames, and other homemade and commercial equipment (see **Sawhorse,** p. 40; **Trestles,** p. 42; and **Cube,** p. 33).

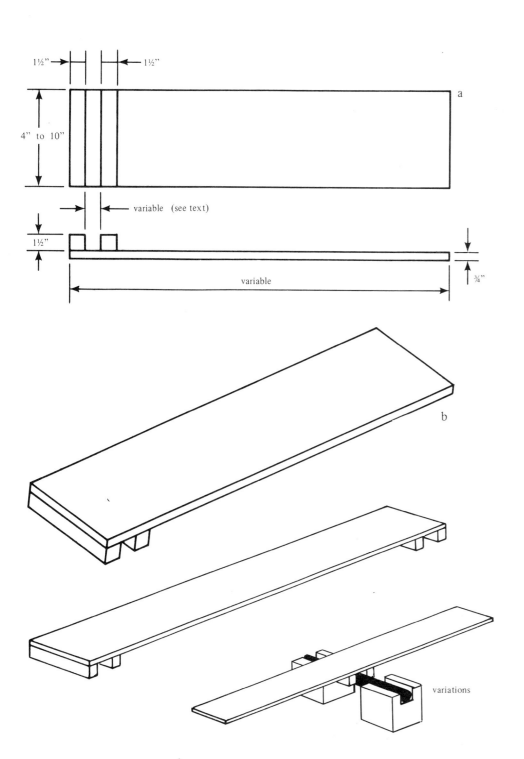

1½"   1½"

a

4" to 10"

variable   (see text)

1½"   ¾"

variable

b

variations

59

Inclined planes

Supplies

Materials

wood—one 4 ft. × 4 ft. sheet of ¾ in. plywood will
      make any two of the diagrammed planes
nails—1 to 1½ in. finishing nails
wood glue
wood filler
paint

Tools

saw, wood rasps, hammer, wood clamps, putty knife,
sandpaper, paintbrush

Construction

Measure and cut the plywood (diagram a). Rasp the back
support piece on the top edge so that it will fit the sloping
board (the angle depends on the height and length of the
unit). Rasp and sand the bottom ends of the base and the
sloping piece to obtain a reasonable fit (diagram b).
Clean all joint surfaces. Glue, nail, and fill all joints (diagram c). Clamp until dry. Fill flaws, sand smooth, and
paint. The base should be clearly marked so it can always
rest on the floor. This piece of equipment has been designed for the base to withstand stress.

Variations

Materials

A plastic coating may prove more durable than paint, in which
case a product such as clear Varathane may be used.

Size

The described units do not need a middle support when used by
children under eight years.

If the span of the slope is increased greatly, it would be advis-
able to include a support at the halfway point. Also, the longer
the unsupported incline, the thicker the wood must be to provide adequate support. To strengthen the right-angle joint between the base and the back, nail and glue a piece of 1×1 in
place.

When making inclined planes of a different size from that described above, the easiest method is to cut and assemble the
base and back, then measure directly the length required for
the slope.

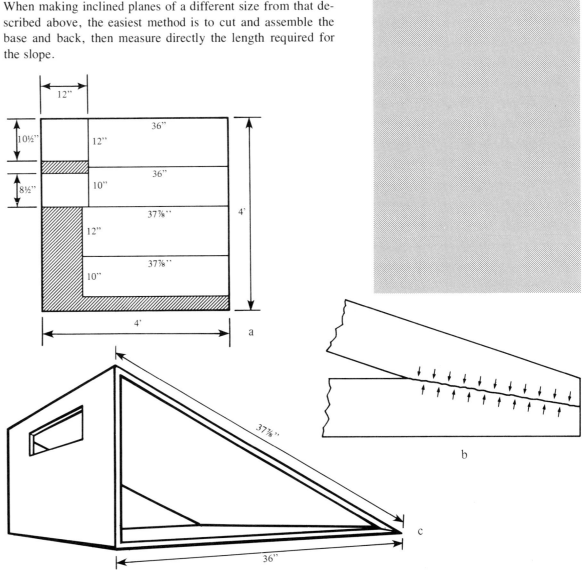

Wooden slide

Supplies

Materials

wood—one 2 ft. × 8 ft. piece of ¾ in. finished
    plywood (slide)
    —two 8 ft. lengths, and one 25½ in. length of 1×3
    finished hardwood (sides and top brace)
    —two 25½ in. lengths of 2×2 hardwood (cleats)
screws—1½ in. wood screws
wood glue
wood filler
paint and varnish

Tools

hand saw, drill, screwdriver, sandpaper, putty knife,
paintbrushes

Construction

Cut the plywood to the above dimensions (diagram a).
Glue the sides and top brace (1×3 hardwood) to the slide
surface. As the glue sets, drill small lead holes along the
side boards and top brace and insert wood screws to
tighten the setting joints (diagram b). Glue and screw the
two lengths of 2×2 onto the underside of the slide top.
The space between these pieces will be determined by the
nature of the supporting structures used for the slide (diagram c). When attaching the sides, top brace, and cleats,
use liberal amounts of glue as it provides the primary
bonding strength. The screws act mainly as clamps. Fill
all flaws. It is most important to sand the slide to a very
smooth finish. Paint, then coat with varnish or Varathane
to increase durability and slipperiness (diagram d).

Variations

Materials

The type of hardwood can vary. The harder woods, mahogany
and walnut, are expensive but are less likely to sliver or
splinter than spruce, fir, or some other softer varieties.

Construction

To avoid problems with slivers, apply a surface of slippery
sheet metal to the slide and turn it under at the bottom. Wood
surfaces can, however, be sliver free if a tough, plasticized finish is applied and renewed from time to time.

The top brace can be omitted if narrower wood (1×2) is used
for the sides.

A riser may be added to the foot of the slide.

Size

The slide could be made longer by splicing together two sections of plywood. In this case, the surface of the slide may
need to be sheet metal to cover the joint.

If the slide is considerably shorter than 8 ft. its usefulness is re-
duced because it can only be raised to a limited extent.

The width of the slide may be changed from the recommended
plans. The minimum width for a slide with sides is 1 ft.

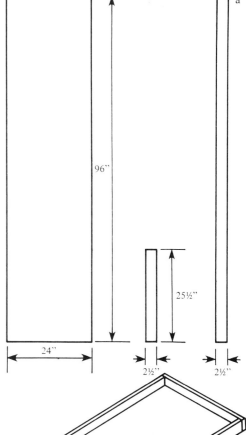

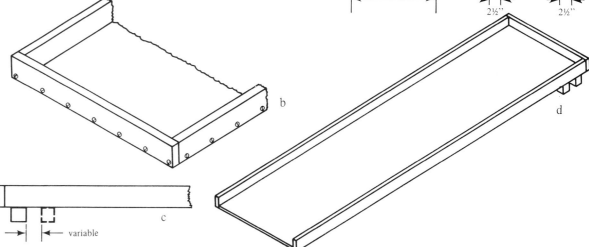

Wooden ladder

Supplies

Materials

wood—one 10 ft. length of 2×4 (makes two 5 ft. legs)
    —six 18 in. pieces of 1 in. diameter dowel (rungs)
    —one 7 in. × 18¾ in. piece of 1 in. plywood
      (top)
screws—1½ in. and 2 in. wood screws
wood glue
wood filler
paint

Tools

saw, drill, screwdriver, clamps, putty knife, sandpaper, paintbrush

Construction

Cut the 2×4 in half, and then cut off the ends (diagram a). Cut the plywood to the size given above. Cut out the corners as shown, to allow for the ladder legs to fit into the plywood piece when the unit is assembled (diagram b). Drill 1 in. diameter holes exactly 1 in. deep into the indicated locations on the legs (diagram c). Glue the ladder rungs to holes into the legs and at the same time glue the plywood top to the inside of the top end of the ladder legs (diagram d). Clamp the entire apparatus until dry, making sure that legs are parallel and even. When dry, drill small lead holes through the edge of the legs into the rungs. Insert 1½ in. wood screws to ensure that rungs will not twist or roll (diagrams e,f). Insert 2 in. screws through the sides of the legs into the edge of the 1 in. plywood catch. Fill, sand, and paint the completed ladder.

Variations

Construction

Cover the feet of the ladder legs with weather mat, rubber stripping, or any other non-slip surface material to prevent floor damage.
Use metal hooks at the top of the ladder instead of the plywood catch. These can be bought or made from bent strap iron.

Size

Space the rungs at irregular intervals.
Vary the length and width of the ladder, but give consideration to other equipment used with the ladder. Both the rung interval and the ladder length should be planned according to the size and ability of the children using it.

Use ladders as bridges. Under these conditions they may need a centre support.

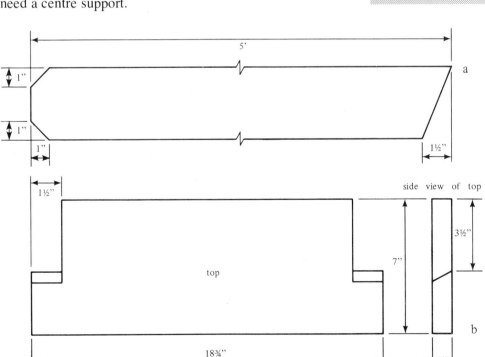

5" 10" 10" 10" 10" 10" 5"

c

d

e

f

63

9 Stilts

Can stilts

Supplies

Materials
two large size, sturdy coffee or juice cans with plastic
   lids
one 6 ft. length of ¼ in. diameter cord
paint

Tools
punch (to make hole slightly larger than ¼ in. diameter)

Construction

Remove all labels from the cans and wash thoroughly.
Puncture two holes on opposite sides of the bottom of
each can (diagram a). Cut the cord into two 3 ft. lengths.
Insert each end of one cord into the holes of one can. Remove the lid from the other end of the can. Pull the ends
through and tie a secure knot (diagram b). Pull the cord
above the two holes on the closed side of the can until the
knot is firmly against the upper lid. Replace the lid on the
lower end of the can. Repeat the procedure for the other
can. Paint or decorate as desired.

Variations

Materials
Vary the type of can.
Construction
When using juice cans do not cut out the bottom. The holes
should be made when first opening the can. To thread the cord,
drill holes ¼ to ½ in. in diameter in the sides of the can near
the top.
Place a plastic lid on both the top and bottom of the cans.
Size and shape
Vary the height and diameter of the cans.
Vary the length of cord to allow different positions of the
arms.

Low, wide cans should be used until children develop
their balance. Then tall, narrow cans can be introduced.
Any cans which warp or bend should be discarded imme-
diately.

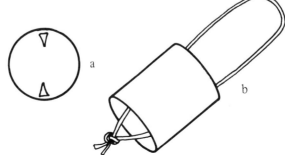

64

Wooden stilts A

Supplies

Materials

wood—one 9 ft. length of 2×2 hardwood (legs)
    —one 6 in. length of 2×4 (footrests)
bolts—two 4 in. long ¼ in. carriage bolts and nuts
    —two 5 in. long ¼ in. carriage bolts and nuts
rubber—two strips approximately 1½ in. × 1½ in.
wood glue
paint or varnish

Tools

saw, drill, ¼ in. drill bit, chisel, wood rasps, screwdriver, wrench or pliers, sandpaper, paintbrush

Construction

Legs

Cut the 2×2 in half. Drill several ¼ in. diameter holes along the stilt legs, spacing them 2 in. apart and starting them 8 in. above the bottom end of the leg (diagram a). Widen the top ¼ in. to recess the bolt heads. Round the top 20 to 30 in. of the legs by rasping and sanding (diagram b). Sand and paint. Glue a small piece of rubber onto the bottom of each leg to prevent them slipping or scratching the floor.

Footrests

Cut the footrests by sawing diagonally across the 6 in. block of 2×4 (diagram c). Drill two parallel holes through each footrest 2 in. apart and along the 6 in. edge. Chisel out small notches so the nuts will sit flat against the wood. Round off the inside points of the footrests (diagram d). Sand and paint.

Assembly

Place the footrest block against stilt leg so that holes correspond. Insert the bolts from the outside to the inside so the nuts will be under each footrest (diagrams d,e).

Variations

Construction

Use a dowel (glued into the step piece) in place of the 4 in. bolt to facilitate changing the step height (diagram f).

When deciding on the thickness of the stilt legs, also consider manoeuverability. Bulky or heavy stilts are awkward for young children to manage.

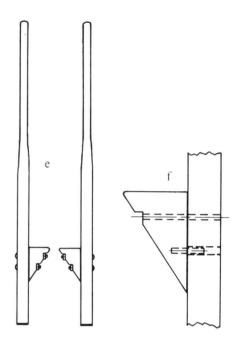

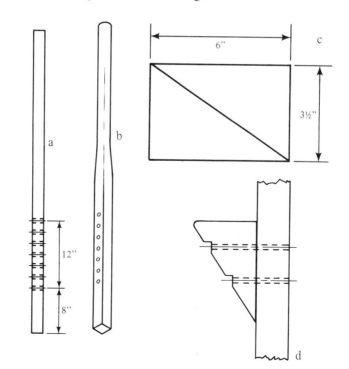

Wooden stilts B

Supplies

Materials

wood—one 10 ft. length of 2×2 hardwood (legs)
    —one 1 ft. length of 2×4 hardwood (footrests)
    —one 1 ft. length of ⅜ in. dowel
rubber—two pieces of thick rubber approximately
        1½ in. × 1½ in.
wood glue
paint or varnish

Tools

same as for **Wooden stilts A,** p. 65

Construction

Legs

Follow the instructions for Wooden stilts A.

Footrests

Saw the 2×4 into two 6 in. pieces. Cut or carve a hole through these blocks 1 in. from the end. The hole must be large enough to allow the footrest to slide down the leg (diagram a). Smooth and sand the hole in the footrests. Paint or varnish.

Assembly

Cut the dowel in half to yield two 6 in. pieces. Check for a snug fit of the dowel in ⅜ in. holes drilled in the legs (if they are loose the footrests will not be held firmly). Place the dowel in the hole corresponding to desired step height and slide the footrest down the leg to rest on the dowel (diagram b). Varnish or paint.

Variations

Materials

The legs can be dowels if strong enough, for example, 1 in. diameter. Dowels supporting the footrests must then be ½ in. diameter or smaller.

Construction

1 in. furniture leg caps can be used to cover the bottom of the stilts if 1 in. dowels are used.

Size

Vary the height of the stilt legs and the interval between dowel holes.

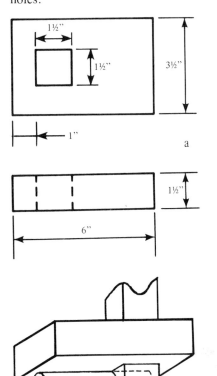

a

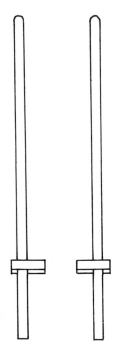

b

Bounce board

Supplies

Materials
wood—one 3 ft. × 4 ft. piece of ½ in. plywood (bounce board)
—about 3 ft. of 2 ×2 hardwood (supports)
screws—1 to 1¼ in. wood screws
wood glue
wood filler
paint

Tools
saw, screwdriver, putty knife, sandpaper, paintbrush

Construction

Cut the bounce board to size. Fill cracks and flaws and sand smooth. Cut the 2×2 into four 9 in. sections. Attach sections to the corners of the underside of the bounce board with glue and wood screws driven through the plywood into the supports (diagram a). Round the corners with sandpaper (diagram b).

Variations

Construction
Change the support system (diagram c). If this is done 6 ft. of support wood will be needed.

Size and shape
Thicker plywood will be required if the size of the bounce board is increased significantly. The bounce board itself can be any of a number of shapes, but the supports should always be placed toward the edges of the board to provide reasonably equal weight bearing on each.

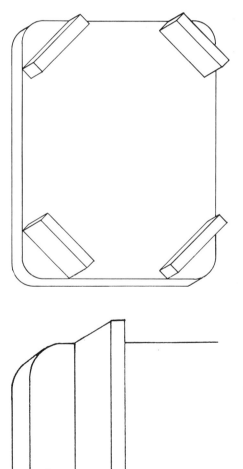

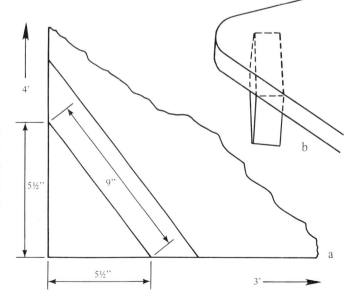

Inner tube bouncer

Supplies

Materials

tire inner tube—approximately 4 ft. 3 in. outside diameter and 9 in. to 10 in. thick when inflated

two pieces of heavy canvas or vinyl coated material, each 4 ft. × 4 ft. (bouncing surfaces)

8 ft. length of 1½ in. wide nylon or cotton webbing

grommets or eyelets

one 36 in. hockey skate lace

heavy thread (buttonhole type)

Tools

sewing machine capable of sewing canvas or hand needles capable of the same work, heavy material shears, grommet or eyelet stapler

Construction

Make each 4 ft. × 4 ft. piece of material into an octagon (diagram a). Sew the edges of the octagons over or sew nylon or vinyl stripping along the edges. Cut the webbing into eight 1 ft. strips, and, if the webbing is nylon, seal with heat to help prevent fraying or splitting. Attach the webbing strips to the corners of the octagon (on either the upper or lower surface) by sewing across the webbing several times (diagram b). Line up the two octagonal surfaces and attach corner-to-corner by the straps (diagram c). Cut a slit approximately 5 in. long above the inner tube valve. Sew several times around this slit, especially at its ends, to prevent tearing or splitting. Using a grommet gun or stapler insert grommets along either side of the slit. Thread the hockey lace (diagram d). Since this cover is permanently attached to the straps, the inner tube must be inflated *after* being fitted into the cover. The air hose is inserted through the slit to reach the valve. The tube is then inflated to an appropriate pressure, the air hose removed, and the slit tightly laced up. Turn the bouncer over so slit is on the bottom side (diagram e).

Variations

Materials

Vary the types of webbing and surface materials according to cost, durability, and availability. The materials must be heavy-duty, however, but can be either non-elastic or stiff elastic.

Construction

One variation that will make inflating the tube easier is to insert grommets on four adjacent corners of the bottom piece. The top section still has all the straps sewn on. Attach strong hooks to the free end of the four straps above the grommets. The tube is inflated, the cover slipped on, and the loose straps hooked into the grommets. No slit is needed in this variation (diagram f).

Size

The size of this piece of equipment will vary with the size of the inner tubes available. Tractor tire inner tubes can have a diameter of up to 7½ ft. and provide an excellent bouncer base. The tubes need not be new and can often be obtained at very nominal cost, or free, from rural service stations and equipment dealers.

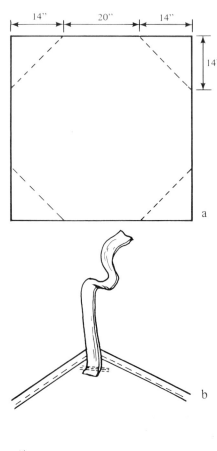

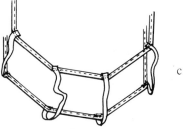

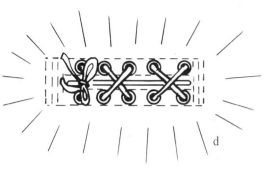

d

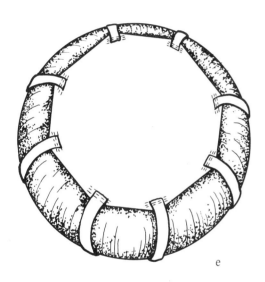

e

Tire bouncer

Supplies

Materials

tire—any size

wood—one piece of 1 in. plywood large enough to overlap the inside tire rim diameter by at least 2 in.
on all sides

bolts—four ¼ in. bolts (length to vary with tire thickness) with matching nuts and wide, steel
washers

wood filler

paint

Tools

jig- or sabre saw, drill, wrench, putty knife, sandpaper,
paintbrush

Construction

Cut a circle from the plywood. The diameter of the circle
should be 4 in. more than the inside tire rim diameter, to
allow 2 in. overlap at all points. Drill ¼ in. diameter
holes at four places on the board edge (1 in. from the
edge) and through corresponding points in the tire (diagram a). Enlarge the top ¼ in. of each hole in the
plywood enough to recess the bolt heads. Fill flaws in the
wood, sand, and paint. Bolt the wood to the tire, placing
washers between the tire and nuts to prevent the nuts
from being pulled through.

Variations

Construction

Two circular boards could be cut and attached to both rims of
the tire.

Size

The tire may range from a small car tire to a tractor tire.

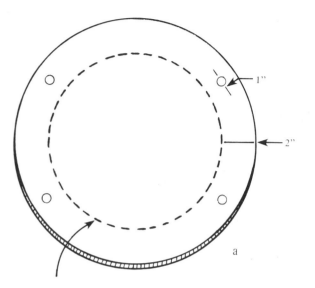

1"

2"

a

inner rim of tire

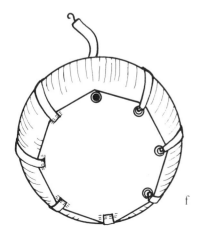

f

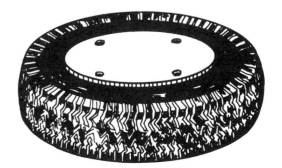

Knotted rope

Supplies

Materials
rope—¾ in. smooth surface rope (finished length plus about 9 in. per knot and 2 ft. for top loop)
athletic tape—one roll
clamp or bracket for top loop

Construction

Make a loop in the top 1 ft. of the rope and close the loop using a squeeze clamp, bracket, or by splicing (diagrams a,b). Tie knots 12 in. apart, starting from the top (diagram c). Tape or seal the end of rope to prevent fraying. Nylon rope can be sealed by touching a hot knife or iron to the end, melting the coating. Suspend the rope by placing the loop around a suspending bar (diagram d) or by hanging the loop over the bar and threading the knotted rope through the loop (diagram e).

Variations

Construction
Tie the knots at more or less than the suggested 1 ft. The knots may also be at irregular intervals.
The rope can be unknotted or a single knot may be at the bottom end.

Size
Vary the length of the rope according to the height needed.
Also vary the rope thickness, using 1½ in. diameter if obtainable.

The method of closing the loop at the top of the rope will vary with the materials and skills available. Splicing is effective if properly done, and splicing instructions are available from rope manufacturing firms. If brackets or clamps are used it is important to have a good length within the clamp and to avoid cutting the rope.

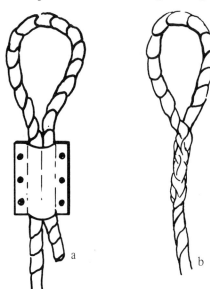

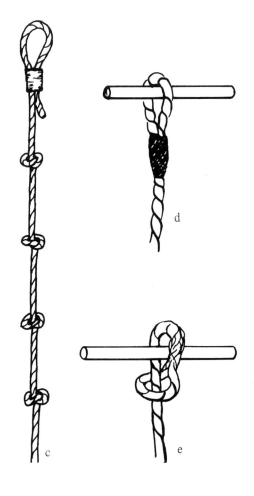

Trapeze

Supplies

Materials

wood—16 in. length of 1 in. hardwood dowel (bar)

rope—½ in. diameter smooth rope (length is height of the supporting bar less the desired distance off the ground for the bar; allow 2 ft. extra for the knots and assembly)

paint or varnish

Tools

saw, drill with ½ in. bit, sandpaper, paintbrush

Construction

Cut the dowel to size. Drill two ½ in. diameter holes through the dowel, locating each hole 1 in. from each end of the dowel and making sure that the holes are parallel to each other (diagram a). Sand and paint or varnish. Thread the two rope ends through the holes in the dowel and knot each end separately (diagrams b,c). To attach the trapeze to a supporting bar, loop the top end of the rope over the supporting bar and pass the trapeze bar through this loop (diagram d).

Variations

Construction

Other methods of attaching the trapeze to the rope include splicing the ends and clamping. Only the least complicated method is discussed here.

Size

Since the trapeze arrangement described is not adjustable, it is necessary to consider carefully the height at which the trapeze is set.

Older children may need thicker rope.

Periodic inspection of the trapeze apparatus is necessary to provide complete safety.

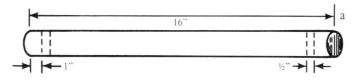

Rope ladder

Supplies

Materials

wood—a number of 16 in. lengths of 1 in. hardwood dowel (total number depends on the height of the support from the floor)

rope—#6 or #10 sashcord, or ⅜ to ½ in. nylon rope (length is at least double the desired height of the ladder, plus 9 to 11 ft.)

twine—nylon or any strong twine (for grooved dowel assembly)

adhesive cloth tape

shellac or varnish

Tools

saw, wood rasp or lathe (for grooved dowels), drill with ¼ in. or ½ in. bit (for drilled dowels), sandpaper, paintbrush

Construction

Tied rung assembly

File and sand rungs smooth, then varnish, shellac, or paint. Double the rope over and attach the top rung at the location indicated (diagram a). Rungs should be no more than 10 in. apart. The knot (diagram b) should be tightened and possibly taped to secure completely. A small wooden plug may be glued into a hole drilled just outside the knot, thereby preventing the knot sliding off the rung (diagram c). The ends of the rope should be spliced, taped, or melted to prevent unravelling or shredding. The ladder is hung with the ladder portion being dropped over the support and through the loop formed by the top of the ladder (diagram d).

Grooved rung assembly

Space the rungs 10 in. apart as in previous assembly. Groove the dowels 1 in. from each end with a wood rasp, lathe, or any other suitable tool (diagram e). Grooves should be about ¼ in. deep. Finish the dowels with sandpaper, and varnish. Using the same initial procedure as for the tied rung assembly, begin by attaching the top rung of ladder (diagram f). Bind with twine, using a figure eight pattern to tighten the rope and dowel joint (diagram g). Use adhesive tape to prevent the twine loosening or unravelling. Hang ladder (diagram d).

Drilled rung assembly

Again use 1 in. dowel rungs 10 in. apart. Extra rope will be needed for the knots. Drill holes through the dowels, 1 in. from each end and just large enough for the rope to pass through. Slide the top rung up the ladder toward the loop. Tie knots under the dowel (diagram h). Continue in this manner until all rungs are in place. Seal or splice the rope ends. Hang the ladder (diagram d).

Variations

Materials

Use any smooth rope or cord, the thickness depending on the size of the children using the ladders.

Size

Vary width of ladder from 12 to 16 in.

Vary the spacing of the rungs. For children under eight years the distance between rungs should be no more than 10 in. Rungs may be irregularly spaced or may be progressively closer together or farther apart as they are set higher or lower on the ladder.

Rope ladders should be checked frequently for rotting, fraying, slipping, or tearing and should be stored in a position which will avoid kinks as much as possible. The emphasis must be on safety and durability, and any design or construction variations should consider these factors.

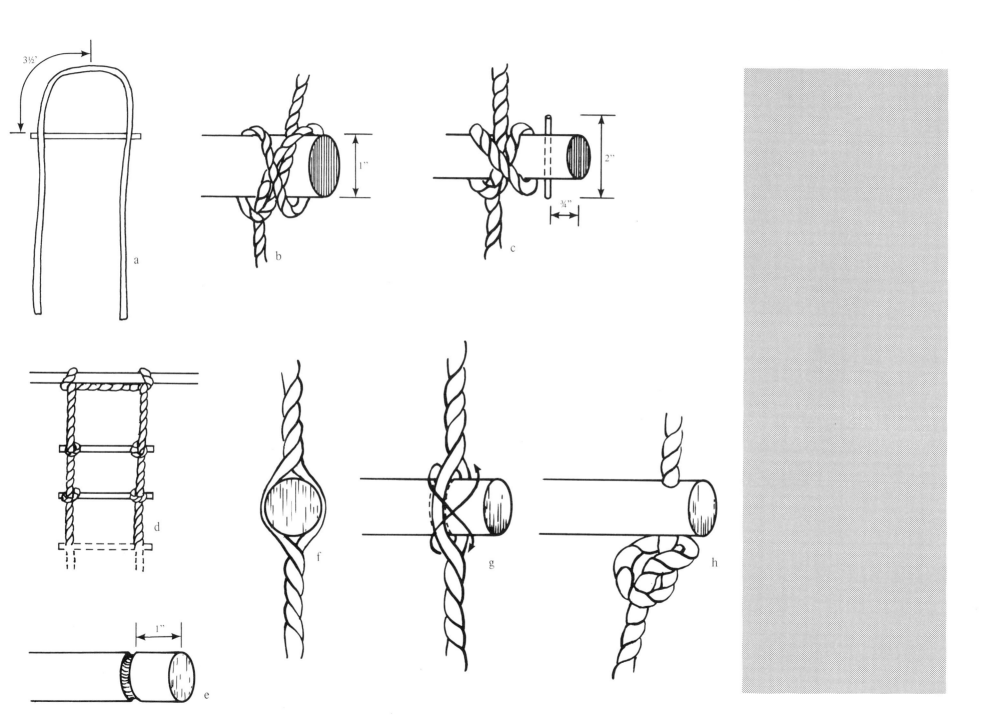

Rings

Supplies

Materials

rope—⅜ to ½ in. nylon or other smooth rope (length is the height of the support bar less the desired distance of the rings above the floor; allow approximately 1½ ft. extra on each rope for the ring loop and splicing)

tubing—approximately 16 in. of rubber or stiff plastic (inside diameter should be slightly larger than the rope)

white cloth adhesive tape

Tools

saw or heavy shears

Construction

Cut the 16 in. length of tubing in half with a saw or shears. Thread the rope through each length of tubing and splice into a loop (diagram a). Clamps may be used if splicing is a problem. Wrap the tubing with the cloth tape to provide a better grip and protect against splitting (diagram b). Splice or clamp the tops of each rope so that rings are suspended independently.

Variations

Construction

There are some types of heavy fibreglass or metal commercial rings which can simply be attached to the ropes. The rings must be continuous, however, so there is no chance of separation during use.

Size

The thickness of the rope may vary, as well as the diameter and type of tubing used. The tubing should be stiff but not so stiff as to crack or split when bent.

A ring diameter of 5 to 6 in. is suitable for use by small children. Additionally, the diameter of the tubing itself should allow a solid grip by young children.

Check frequently for cracking or splitting of the ring and fraying or rotting of the ropes.

74

Swing

Supplies

Materials
wood—6 in. × 16 in. piece of ¾ in. hardwood or plywood (seat)
rope—¾ in. (double height desired, plus 3 ft.)
wood filler
paint

Tools
drill, ¾ in. bit, putty knife, sandpaper, paintbrush

Construction

Drill four ¾ in. diameter holes through the swing seat (diagram a). Round the seat corners with sandpaper. Fill any cracks or flaws, sand thoroughly, and paint or varnish. Thread the rope through holes in the seat and splice, braid, or clamp so that the seat is supported by rope at equal heights on both sides (diagram b). Splice or clamp loops at the top ends of the ropes to accommodate the support bar, or loop the uncut rope over the bar as shown.

Variations

Materials
Use a rubber or canvas sling for the seat.
Construction
If a sling is used, grommets or eyelets must be inserted to attach the rope.
Supporting ribs may be added lengthways to the underside of a wooden swing seat.
Size
Vary the size of the swing according to the children using it.

a

1"
1"

splices

b

Disc swing

Supplies

Materials
wood—10 in. circle of ¾ in. plywood
rope—¾ in. nylon (desired length plus 1 ft.)
wood filler
paint or varnish

Tools
drill with ¾ in. bit, jig- or sabre saw, sandpaper, putty knife, paintbrush

Construction

Cut a 10 in. diameter circle from the plywood (diagram a). Drill a ¾ in. diameter hole through the centre of the circle. Fill and sand, rounding seat edges carefully. Paint. Tie a knot or double knot in the end of the rope and thread the other end through the hole in swing (diagram b). Slide the swing seat down to the knot. Splice, clamp, or otherwise make a permanent loop in the top 1 ft. of the rope (diagram c).

Variations

Materials
Use an old frisbee.
Construction
Cover the swing seat with an old rubber disc or frisbee, or pad with foam and cover with vinyl.

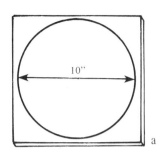
10"
a

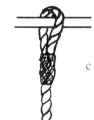
b

c

Swinging plank

Supplies

Materials

wood—5 ft. × 10 in. piece of ¾ in. plywood or hard-
    wood (plank)
    —40 in. of 2×2 hardwood (cleats)
rope—about 14 ft. of ¾ in. nylon or manilla
wood glue
wood filler
nails—1¼ in. finishing (or wood screws)
paint

Tools

saw, hammer or screwdriver, drill with ¾ in. bit, large
shears or knife, putty knife, sandpaper, paintbrush

Construction

Cut the 2×2 into four 10 in. lengths. Using glue and
nails, attach the 10 in. lengths to the plank (diagram a).
The space between the cleats should be ¾ in. to 1 in.
wide. Fill all flaws, sand thoroughly, and paint. Cut the
rope in half. How you attach these two sections to the
supporting equipment will vary with the nature of the
supporting bar. The rope can be tied, hooked onto commercial hooks which are in the supporting bar, or pulled
through a drilled hole and tied to a dowel (diagram b).
However, in all cases the suspending ropes must angle
slightly outwards from the seat. This ensures the stability
of the plank (diagram c).

Variations

Construction

Instead of using cleats to stabilize the rope, drill holes about

1 in. from each plank edge and thread the rope through these
holes and under the plank (diagram c).

Size

Vary the thickness of the rope according to the weight of the
children, or use chain.
Vary wood plank thickness and dimensions from narrow, such
as a 1×4 or 2×4, to wide, such as a 1×8 or 2×6. Adjust the
suspending ropes to suit the type of plank or board used.

If sawhorses or other A frames are used to support the
plank, it is important to position them close enough together to let the plank hang directly below the support
bars. This will prevent the A frames from tipping over.

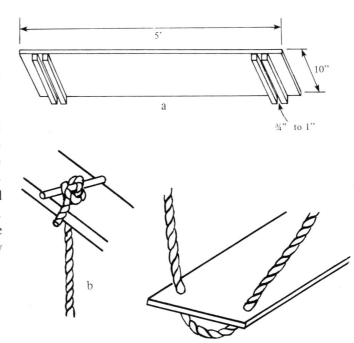